SCHOLASTIC

100 ART & DESIGN LESSONS

Terms and conditions

IMPORTANT – PERMITTED USE AND WARNINGS – READ CAREFULLY BEFORE USING

This CD-ROM has been tested for viruses at all stages of its production. However, we recommend that you run virus-checking software on your computer systems at all times. Scholastic Ltd cannot accept any responsibility for any loss, disruption or damage to your data or your computer system that may occur as a result of using either the CD-ROM or the data held on it.

IF YOU ACCEPT THE ABOVE CONDITIONS YOU MAY PROCEED TO USE THE CD-ROM.

Recommended system requirements:

- Windows: XP (Service Pack 3), Vista (Service Pack 2) or Windows 7 with 2.33GHz processor
- Mac: OS 10.6 to 10.8 with Intel Core™ Duo processor
- 1GB RAM (recommended)
- 1024 x 768 Screen resolution
- CD-ROM drive (24x speed recommended)
- 16-bit sound card
- Microsoft Word

For all technical support queries, please phone Scholastic Customer Services on 0845 6039091.

SCHOLASTIC

Book End, Range Road, Witney, Oxfordshire, OX29 0YD
www.scholastic.co.uk

3 4 5 6 7 8 9   8 9 0 1 2 3

British Library Cataloguing-in-Publication Data
A catalogue record for this book is available from the British Library.

ISBN 978-1407-14086-5
Printed by Bell & Bain Ltd, Glasgow

Authors
Laurence Keel and Julia Stanton

Editorial
Robin Hunt and Sara Wiegand

Cover Design
Nicolle Thomas

Design Team
Nicolle Thomas and Black Dog Design

Illustrations
Moreno Chiacchiera (Beehive illustration)

Contents

Introduction

Art and design is a subject full of opportunities for children to develop their creativity and skills. In the classroom teachers endeavour to engage, inspire and challenge children, in addition to equipping them with the knowledge and skills to experiment, invent and create their own works of art, craft and design. As children progress, they will be encouraged to think critically, reflect upon their own work and the work of their classmates to enable them to grow and further enhance their creativity.

The National Curriculum for art & design aims to ensure that all pupils:
- *produce creative work, exploring their ideas and recording their experiences*
- *become proficient in drawing, painting, sculpture and other art, craft and design techniques*
- *evaluate and analyse creative works using the language of art, craft and design*
- *know about great artists, craft makers and designers, and understand the historical and cultural development of their art forms.*

It is hoped that this planning resource will provide a dynamic planning framework which evolves in the classroom, with teachers adapting and developing the ideas in each unit of work. The framework is divided into six units for each school year, providing coverage of the National Curriculum aims and objectives, encompassing the required skills and understandings and a range of teaching and learning approaches. Teachers are encouraged to extend the learning where possible to encompass visits to exhibitions and galleries, group projects and other cross-curricular opportunities or to adapt the units for another year group.

In this planning guide, the National Curriculum aims have informed the long-term planning:

- ***Explore and create*** KS1: using a range of materials to design and make products; using drawing, painting and sculpture to share their ideas, experiences and imagination.
  KS2: to experiment and become increasingly aware of different kinds of art, craft and design; to create sketch books to record their observations and collect visual material to help them to develop their ideas.
- ***Skills and techniques*** KS1: developing techniques in using colour, pattern, texture, line, shape, form and space using clay and printing to a large scale and in 3D.
  KS2: to develop their techniques, including control and use of materials; to improve their mastery of techniques, such as drawing, painting and sculpture with materials.
- ***Evaluate and analyse*** KS1: recording their ideas and experiences and talking time to review and revisit their ideas.
  KS2: use their sketch books and (recorded) observations to review and revisit ideas.
- ***Art and artists*** KS1: being taught about the work of a range of artists, craft makers, and designers, describing the differences and similarities between different practices and disciplines, and making links to their own work.
  KS2: about the greatest artists, architects and designers in history.

Terminology

In this guide, the main terms used are:

- ***Outcomes***: Learning outcomes are the skills and knowledge which it is intended that children should be able to demonstrate at the end of the lesson or unit of work.
- ***Objectives***: By the end of Key Stage 1 and Key Stage 2, children are expected to know, apply and understand the matters, skills and processes.
- ***Skills and understanding***: Art & design skills which may need specific teaching or emphasis.
- ***Areas of study***: It is suggested that children are taught through the six key areas of teaching and learning – drawing, painting, printing, sculpture, collage and textiles. Digital media is not a separate area of study, but should be integrated into the other six areas.

Assessment

Throughout the units it is suggested that teachers should provide opportunities for children, and teachers, to discuss and evaluate their creative output, their mastery of skills and techniques and increasing knowledge, and that of their peers and be able to suggest future improvements. It is recommended that schools create a file of children's work to help benchmark achievements and progress. There are many examples of child self-evaluation rubrics which can be used to help children focus on their developing skills, although individual and class discussions can be equally, if not more, valuable. A template for teacher assessment is on the CD-ROM, along with a completed example.

Materials (Equipment)

Required materials are mentioned throughout the planning guide. However, as it is important to have all materials in advance, a comprehensive list for each unit is available on the CD-ROM.

Health & safety

It is important to ensure the health and safety of children and adults at all times and for teachers and coordinators therefore to identify and resolve any potential risks. Particular care should be taken when using tools which may be heavy, pointed, sharp or hot and to ensure that there is a suitable level of adult supervision of any electrical tools. Encourage children to understand potential risks and care for their own safety. NSEAD publish a *Guide to Safe Practice in Art and Design*, which might be useful for this purpose.

About the book

The book provides content for each year group (Y1–6) and includes:

- ***Long-term planning***: An overview of the areas of study (aims) and the National Curriculum objectives for that year (based upon the statutory guidance from the curriculum – in black text (DfE, 2013) and supporting non-statutory guidance from other LA support documents – in grey text).
- ***Overview of progression***: A year-by-year overview of how the children progress through the art & design skills and understanding.
- ***Medium-term planning***: Six half-termly grids are provided for each year group. Each contains a weekly overview including the theme covered, outcomes for that week and the objectives, skills and media covered.
- ***Background knowledge***: This explains key concepts, relevant to the year group, to support teachers' knowledge of art & design in relation to the units.

About the CD-ROM

The CD-ROM provides the long-term planning, progression, medium-term planning, background knowledge and materials lists as editable Word files. A teacher assessment grid, that can be used and adapted to meet the needs of your classroom, and a completed example, are also included. Design templates, mentioned in the sessions, are also provided. From the menu screen on the CD-ROM, simply navigate to the year group you require and then click on the button to open the associated file. Visit **www.scholastic.co.uk/100artanddesign** for some additional resources linked to the contents of this book.

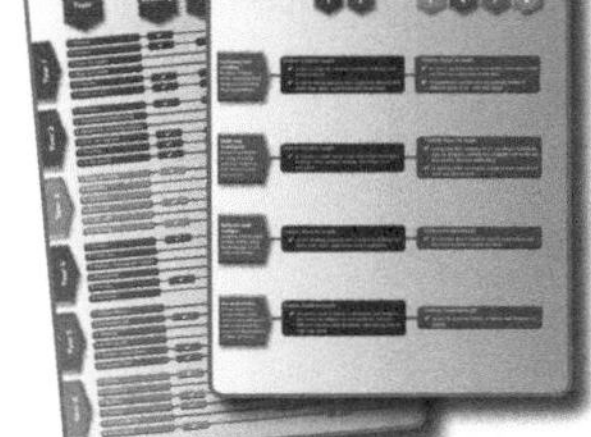

About the poster

The poster summarises the progression of key concepts, skills and techniques in the National Curriculum. Display in a central location, such as the staffroom, to help improve understanding of the new curriculum within your school.

Year 1 Long-term planning

Aim 1: Exploring and creating

The National Curriculum states that children should be taught:

- to use a range of materials creatively to design and make products.
- to use drawing, painting and sculpture to... share their ideas, experiences and imagination.

Making and recording observations first hand and from memory.

Developing their ideas, trying things out and asking questions.

Exploring thoughts and ideas using their experience, imagination and originality through a range of creative opportunities.

Children experience and learn about:

- drawing to express different weather conditions
- the art found in gardens
- a range of printing techniques
- exploring 2D and 3D sculptures
- a range of firework collages
- creating a collaborative collage.

Aim 2: Skills and techniques

The National Curriculum states that children should be taught:

- to develop... techniques in using colour, pattern, texture, line, shape, form and space.

To experience and develop techniques in drawing, painting, sculpture and collage with a variety of materials and tools including ICT. Children develop their artistic techniques in:

- drawing from observation, memory and imagination
- painting using a range of media and combining different media
- a range of printing methods
- creating sculpted animals
- cutting and arranging paper to make compositions
- creating collage by combining a range of different materials and media
- using a range of arts and craft materials to apply finishes to their work.

Work safely with a range of tools and techniques, including appropriate new technology tools, taking care of themselves and others.

Aim 3: Evaluate and analyse

The National Curriculum states that children should be taught:

- to use drawing, painting and sculpture to develop and share their ideas, experiences and imagination.

Reflect on what they and others have done and say what they think and feel about it.

Suggest ways in which they might change or develop their work.

Throughout the units of work children should be encouraged to record, annotate and modify their work as often as possible creating a personal source of information and ideas, including:

- talking about their work and how they achieved it
- developing an appropriate vocabulary
- trying out different ideas and designs
- identifying ways in which their work can be improved upon
- talk about and give opinions on the work of others.

Aim 4: Art and artists

The National Curriculum states that children should be taught:

- about the work of a range of artists, craft makers and designers, describing the differences and similarities between different practices and disciplines, and making links to their own work.

Learn about, understand and value the work of artists, craft makers and designers; the differences and similarities between them and making links to their own work.

Children learn about the works of a range of artists, including:

- John Constable
- Andy Goldsworthy
- Pablo Picasso
- Richard Long
- Rebecca Coles.

Overview of progression in Year 1

Throughout the units in Year 1, children are:

- Making and recording observations, both first-hand observations and from memory.
- Exploring and developing their ideas and experiences, using their imagination and originality through a range of creative opportunities.
- Learning about, understanding and valuing the work of artists, craft makers and designers; the differences and similarities between them and making links to their own works.
- Reflecting on what they and others have done and say what they think and feel about it and suggest ways in which they might change or develop their work.

Drawing

Through drawing to reflect different weather conditions, children are:

- Drawing on different surfaces and with a range of media.
- Experimenting to create different lines and marks made with a range of media.
- Drawing lines and shapes from observations of nature and objects.
- Investigating textures by copying patterns.

Through studying about gardens, children are:

- Experimenting to create different lines and marks made with a range of media.
- Drawing lines and shapes from observations of nature and objects.

Through exploration of art around firework and under the sea themes, children are:

- Drawing on different surfaces and with a range of media.
- Experimenting to create different lines and marks made with a range of media.
- Drawing lines and shapes from observations of nature and objects.

Painting

Through studying about gardens, children are:

- Using a variety of paint media and experimenting to produce a range of effects.
- Using a variety of tools and techniques including different brushes and investigating the kinds of marks which can be made.
- Identifying primary colours and undertaking simple colour-mixing to include shades and tones.
- Matching colours to artefacts and objects.
- Naming different types of paint and their properties.

Through studying different weather conditions, children are:

- Identifying primary colours and undertaking simple colour-mixing to include shades and tones.

Through exploration of art around a firework theme, children are:

- Using a variety of paint media and experiments to produce a range of effects.
- Using a variety of tools and techniques including different brushes and investigating the kinds of marks which can be made.

Year 1 Complete 'Overview of progression' is provided on the CD-ROM, including 'Printing', 'Collage and textiles' and 'Sculpture' objectives.

Medium-term planning: 1. Weather

YEAR 1

This unit of work is a series of drawing activities that encourage children to develop their skills and techniques around a common theme of weather.

W	Outcomes	Objectives	Skills and understanding
1	**Exploring weather** • Can create a response drawing using a range of media and papers to express feelings about weather.	• To respond to what is observed • To draw on different surfaces with a range of media including: pencils, crayons, pastels and chalk • To experiment to create different lines and marks made with a range of media	Explore, through discussion, how weather impacts our moods and behaviour. Use different paper, e.g. colours, to depict seasons; and a choice of media to depict weather effects – including dots, dashes, sweeping and wavy lines. Experiment with weight of line and a range of colour combinations.
2	**Wind and movement** • Can draw wind-blown objects to reflect sound and movement with lines and marks.	• To observe and identify key qualities of natural and seen objects, represent lines and shapes	Outside, observe how wind changes natural and man-made objects. Record sound and movement with pencils and charcoal on sketchpads. Encourage working at larger scale if possible.
3	**It's raining!** • Can complete a sequence of rain drawings using line and wash to show increasing intensity.	• To experiment to create different lines and marks made with a range of media, showing evidence of increasing control • To identify primary colours	Discuss how to depict rain of different intensity, using varying weight and type of line. Begin with paper folded in three sections. Create three different drawings showing rain increasing in intensity; when paper is unfolded it shows a rain sequence. Add wash in primary colour.
4	**Sun and shadows** • Can create a group drawing showing an overlapping composition.	• To develop confidence in recording their first-hand observations • To work together in a small group to create a joint composition	Outside, or with a strong light source, observe shadows created by children or man-made objects. Draw around shadows on large sheets of paper in small groups. Move objects to create overlap or use different objects to create overlap.
5	**Clouds** • Can identify and talk about types of clouds.	• To draw clouds using a range of media • To develop confidence in their ability to draw things they observe and develop technique to represent them • To use different surfaces with a range of media to increase recognition • To explore the work of great artists in history	Reflect on clouds in artists' work (see 'Background knowledge') and record clouds over time. Return to artists' work at end of session, to make links to children's work. Draw a range of clouds using different media to depict: charcoal for rain; pastels for sunny day. Texture can be added for class display.
6	**Autumn leaves** • Can copy leaf patterns and create own patterned and textured leaf drawings.	• To create prints from found leaves • To develop and refine their control over a variety of drawing tools and media • To reflect on what they have done and suggest ways to change or develop their work • To use a range of found objects to make prints	Observe and collect a range of autumn leaves. Cut some of the leaves in half and paste to paper; add pattern and texture to create the other half. Record patterns and textures of found leaves, choosing some to use for printing. Use drawings and prints to create a class collage, inspired by Andy Goldsworthy.

Notes:
Digital: Use a digital camera to record explorations and investigations by children, for reference and to incorporate into classroom displays.
This unit provides opportunities for cross-curricular work in Year 1 science on seasonal changes.

Medium-term planning: 2. Gardens

This unit of work offers a series of activities that introduce and develop a range of skills and techniques using paint around a common theme of gardens.

W	Outcomes	Objectives	Skills and understanding
1	**Mark making** • Can create a range of marks, using imagination in the use of tools to illustrate garden shapes, colours and textures.	• To experiment with a variety of painting implements to investigate the kinds of marks they make • To use painting techniques to respond to what is seen, remembered or imagined	Explore, through discussion, the colours, shapes and textures found in gardens. Use a range of objects: forks, scourers, a nail brush, some bubble wrap, a potato masher, other everyday objects as painting tools. Use only primary colours.
2	**Print and paint flowers** • Can use primary colours to create flowers using paint on parts of hands and paintbrushes.	• To experiment with paint and investigate the kinds of marks made • To explore the work of great artists in history	Discuss how to make paint thinner or thicker, experiment using primary colours. Create a range of flower heads with the use of each child's whole hand, adding stalks afterwards. Using the same colours create flowers using paintbrushes with flat edges; discuss the differences between the flowers.
3	**Flower wheel** • Can work with a partner to create a colour wheel using paint and petals.	• To identify primary colours and know about simple colour mixing	Provide pairs of children with a paper plate segmented into six. Display and discuss a colour wheel. Using paintbrushes with flat edges, add large swatches of each primary colour (mixed with glue) to the appropriate segment on the plates. Carefully mix the two relevant primary colours to make the three complementary colours, adding a large swatch of these colours to the plates. Add petals to decorate their plate, matching to the appropriate segment, making a colour wheel.
4	**Abstract flowers** • Can create an abstract flower print showing different tints, using only two primary colours.	• To know about simple colour mixing and shading • To take a simple print	Provide two primary colours each with white paint and water – vary the two colours. Encourage children to experiment, mixing the colours and making marks to display the variety. Add white paint to show different tints. Fold square sheets of paper in half. Using paintbrushes with flat edges and a range of colours create an abstract shape on half the sheet. Fold the blank half over the paint, to create an abstract flower when opened.
5	**Lupins** • Can create a flower using paint to print petals showing shade and texture.	• To experiment with a variety of painting and printing techniques to investigate the kinds of marks which can be made • To use painting techniques to respond to what is seen, remembered or imagined	Explore, through discussion, the colours, shapes, leaves and textures found on lupins. Add a wash background to sugar paper and add green stalk/s. Use finger and/or thumb prints in chosen colour to create flowers. Use only one colour and white to provide shading.
6	**Spiral – trails and paths** • Can create an abstract painting with a spiral shape using a range of techniques.	• To experiment to create geometric lines and shapes • To undertake simple colour-mixing to include shades and tones • To experiment with different media	Divide class into two groups. *Snail trail*: Provide A4 black card. Use white chalk to draw a snail trail spiral; paint over the trail with a neutral paint shade (mix glue in the paint); add glitter to finish. Garden path: Provide A3 white card. Draw a large spiral using string which is glued to the card; make thumb prints stepping stones, in primary colours, within the spiral; outline stones in black for effect.

Notes:
Session 2: Search online for 'Picasso + Flowers in Hand' to view images of Picasso's *Flowers in Hand* painting as a stimulus; make links to children's own work.

Medium-term planning: 3. From the toy box

This unit of work comprises activities that introduce and develop a range of printing skills and techniques using items from the toy box and the art store.

W	Outcomes	Objectives	Skills and understanding
1	**Exploring prints** • Can experiment to create a range of prints using lots of different printing tools.	• To make patterns and pictures by printing with objects both natural and man-made • To use appropriate vocabulary to describe printing and patterns	Use a range of items from the toy box, dipped in paint, to make patterns and marks on papers – cars to make trails, Multilink to make shapes etc. Experiment with different paints, but keep range small and consider different coloured paper. Discuss the prints made and encourage children to guess which items created which prints.
2	**Wrap it up** • Can create a print from an entire object.	• To make patterns and pictures by printing with objects both natural and man-made	Explore, through discussion, the effect of applying paint to all surfaces of an item – a toy car, a LEGO tree. Carefully apply paint to all surfaces then wrap in paper; unwrap and discuss the print.
3	**Bouncing balls** • Can create a range of prints, understanding the transfer process and the effect of multiple prints.	• To make patterns and pictures by printing with objects both natural and man-made	Outside, or in a wet area, lay down large sheets of white or black paper. Apply paint, from a range determined by base colour, to the surface of a small range of balls – basketballs, tennis balls etc. Bounce the balls on the paper, randomly or on the same spot with multiple applications of paint and observe and discuss the results.
4	**Shoe prints** • Can use imagination to create a print design, displaying increasing printing skills.	• To use a block to make a simple press print • To create different simple designs by experimenting with overprinting, motifs and colour patterns	Use the soles of dolls shoes from the toy box as a simple block. Create overprinted patterns with a range of colours, considering how the colour will be used in the pattern – contrasting or complementary. Children can bring an old shoe to school to use as a printing block.
5	**Boxes & blocks** • Can create a print design displaying a variety of repeating patterns.	• To create different simple designs by experimenting with repeating patterns • To explore the work of great artists in history	Experiment with matchboxes and wooden blocks. How many prints can be made using all faces of the items? Make a range of prints then move on to create repeating patterns with varying incidences of repeats. Use prints of different shapes to create a robot print than add detail with felt-tipped pens.
6	**Mono-print** • Can use experience and imagination to create a work with a central print using a range of tools.	• To use a block to make a simple mono-print • To use a roller and simple printing palette	Cut a shape to use as a printing block from heavy cardboard. (This may have to be done by an adult.) Wrap the cardboard with a piece of bubble wrap and secure behind the 'block'. Ink the block, using a single colour and take a print. Use the print as the centre of an imaginative animal or plant; use drawing or painting skills to add details.

Notes:

Use a digital camera to record explorations and investigations by children for reference and to incorporate into classroom displays.

Session 5: Look at the prints using hands from Richard Long @ www.richardlong.org or on the Tate website; make links to children's own work.

Medium-term planning: 4. Bugs and beetles

This unit of work offers a series of activities that introduce and develop a range of sculpting skills and techniques with malleable materials around a common theme of bugs.

W	Outcomes	Objectives	Skills and understanding
1	**Exploring Plasticine®** • Can use imagination to create patterns and shapes in Plasticine®, using hands and other tools.	• To manipulate malleable materials in a variety of ways to produce imaginative creations with hands and found objects	Explore the properties of Plasticine®, using hands to manipulate and create shapes, discussing the process and the outcomes. Roll the Plasticine® into a smooth shape. Use the rolled shape as a palette for patterns created by hand, fingers and other found objects.
2	**Making bugs** • Can use the materials provided to create a bug sculpture.	• To manipulate malleable materials and use simple techniques to join materials • To use different construction materials creatively to make 3D models	Through observation and discussion, explore the features, shape and colours of a variety of bugs. Use Plasticine® to create the body. Join two pieces with a matchstick as added support if necessary. Have a range of craft materials (beads, buttons, pipe cleaners) to add legs, eyes, antennae.
3	**Texture with clay** • Can use experiences or imagination to create a textured, patterned bug shell with clay.	• To manipulate malleable materials in a variety of ways to produce imaginative creations with hands and found objects • To use a range of tools safely when making models and sculptures	Explore, through discussion, the texture and patterns seen on the bodies of a variety of beetles. Using a ball of clay, rolled into a flat oval shape, create observed, or imagined, textures and patterns with a variety of tools. Small feet and a tail made of clay can be added using the 'scratch and slip' method.
4	**Butterflies** • Can use clay to create a butterfly body, adding features with additional materials.	• To manipulate malleable materials in a variety of ways to produce imaginative creations with hands and found objects • To use different construction materials creatively to make 3D models	Identify the actual shape of a butterfly body; discuss ways in which it can be created from clay, and how to use materials to complete it. Sculpt the body, and head, from a piece of clay, including indentations for eyes, leaving two pencil holes through the shape. Add legs, eyes and antenna and when dry, paint body with paint and other materials. Use crepe paper for wings, pushing through holes then extending.
5	**Snails** • Can use experience of working with clay to create and decorate a snail shape.	• To manipulate malleable materials in a variety of ways to produce imaginative creations with hands and found objects • To use simple techniques to join materials	Using a piece of rolled clay, shape a snail body; separately using another piece of rolled clay create a coil for the snail shell and attach to body using the 'scratch and slip method'. Use ceramic tools to create a patterned spiral texture on the shell. Splatter paint the completed body, and then add materials for the antennae and eyes.
6	**Caterpillars** • Can create a sculpture by joining recycled materials together.	• To use different construction materials creatively to make 3D models • To use simple techniques to join materials and make 3D constructions	Create a sculpture of a caterpillar using recycled egg cartons. Each egg receptacle is cut out to form a segment of the caterpillar body. Glue or staple them together, with help of an adult. The body is painted using bright colours in a regular pattern. Plastic eyes are added and pipe cleaners are used to form the legs.

Notes:
This unit provides opportunities for cross-curricular work in Year 1 science on the comparison of common animals.

Medium-term planning: 5. Fireworks

YEAR 1

This unit of work offers a series of activities that introduce and develop a range of collage and textile skills and techniques around a common theme of fireworks.

W	Outcomes	Objectives	Skills and understanding
1	**Splat!** • Can use different paint techniques to apply paint to paper giving the appearance of fireworks.	• To use painting tools and techniques to respond to what is seen, remembered or imagined	Explore, through discussion, how fireworks look, sound and make you feel and the different ways of representing them. Blow painting: Using large sheets of paper, in pairs, drop blobs of bright colours then blow through a straw for effect. Encourage some overprinting.
2	**Sparkling spirals** • Can create a night scene, incorporating glittering shapes and paper rockets.	• To use a range of materials to make a collage (arrange and glue) • To cut shapes, from a variety of materials and arrange to create either an abstract or representational picture	Draw a range of spirals and stars on a dark background, using bright paint containing glue. Lightly cover paper with glitter and shake off excess leaving glitter design. When dry, add other decorations such as gummed stars and pastel stars and swirls. Add rockets made of different coloured gummed paper.
3	**Scratch fireworks** • Can use a range of techniques to create a fireworks image with vibrant colour.	• To use painting tools and techniques to respond to what is seen, remembered or imagined • To combine different media to create different artistic effects	Crayon etching: Use bright crayons or oil pastels to completely cover an A4 sheet of paper with bright designs, swirls and stripes. Then cover the whole sheet with thick black paint. When completely dry, carefully scrape through the black paint, with lollipop sticks or scrapers, in spirals, splashes and other shapes, revealing the colours below.
4	**Rockets** • Can use a range of techniques to create a 3D sculpture, incorporating textiles.	• To sort materials to make a collage • To learn about different types, colours and textures of fabrics	Use a cardboard tube and circle of cardboard (for the top) to create a rocket. Sort materials to choose appropriate pieces to add to rocket, before adding paper streamers, foil, stars and other textured material for the rocket stream. Rockets can be added to wall frieze or hung from ceilings.
5	**Foil etching** • Can make a foil firework etching, showing care and imagination.	• To apply appropriate decoration to work • To combine different media to create different artistic effects	Tape thick tin foil to pieces of cardboard. Using tempera paint in a dark colour, with a couple of drops of washing-up liquid, cover the foil with paint and leave to dry. Use a lollipop stick to carefully scrape a design into the paint, incorporating rockets, stars, spirals and planets.
6	**Fire collage** • Can make a fire collage using papers and natural objects.	• To sort and choose materials to make a collage • To tear and cut different papers – fold, crumple, tear and overlap papers • To work safely with a range of tools and techniques	Discuss the sights and sounds of a bonfire – what colours do you think of? Look at and feel different types of paper and discuss if the papers look or sound like the memory of a bonfire. From a range of materials (including twigs and textiles) create a collage 'wood pile'. Add collage of fire from a range of different papers and cellophane.

Notes:

This unit of work provides opportunities for cross-curricular work on the Gunpowder Plot, Bonfire Night, Diwali, Chinese New Year and New Year's Eve celebrations around the world.

The unit also provides opportunities to explore the work of great artists describing differences and similarities, see 'Background knowledge' section for suggestions.

See also 'Fireworks Display' on the Scholastic website (www.scholastic.co.uk/100artanddesign)

Medium-term planning: 6. Under the sea

This unit of work is a series of activities on the theme of the sea, bringing together a number of different skills and techniques. The outcomes from each session are used to create a whole class 'Under the sea' display.

W	Outcomes	Objectives	Skills and understanding
1	**What colour is the sea?** • Can respond to images of the sea to create a seascape showing depth.	• To experiment to create different lines and marks made with a range of media	Explore photographs or paintings of the sea, focusing on the changing colour depending on the depth of the water. In pairs, using large sheets of paper, paint wavy lines of blues, greens and whites in layers. Starting with darker wavy lines at the bottom and getting lighter. (These will form the backdrop of the final display.)
2	**Coral** • Can draw and then create textured coral on a background.	• To draw lines and shapes from observations of nature and objects • To use a variety of paint media and experiment to produce a range of effects	Explore photographs of different coral focusing on shape, colour and texture. Draw some coral shapes on sugar paper and cut out. Add colour and texture by gluing coloured rice to the cut-out coral shapes.
3	**Seahorses** • Can use a template and tissue paper to create a rainbow seahorse.	• To tear and cut different papers to make a collage • To arrange and glue materials appropriately	Use a template for the seahorse shape, taking scale of the final piece into consideration. Create different colour effects by overlapping layers of tissue paper on to the seahorse cut-outs. Create additional patterns on each seahorse with glue and add glitter to finish.
4	**Fish** • Can respond to images of fish to create their own fish drawings, creating texture and pattern and choosing colour.	• To draw on different surfaces with a range of media including: pencils, crayons, pastels and chalk • To experiment to create different lines and marks made with a range of media	Explore the different types of fish under the sea: do they have fins and tails; do they have stripes or patterns; what shapes and colours are they? Draw outline shapes before using pencils or paint to add colour, pattern and texture (scales etc.) and other materials for decoration. (Think about scale.)
5	**Giant squid** • Can respond with imagination to draw an underwater animal for their collage.	• To experiment to create different lines and marks using a range of media • To draw lines and shapes from observations of nature • To arrange and glue materials and add appropriate decoration	Display images of giant squid and after a discussion about the shape – big eyes, pointed head, 'blob-like' body and lots of tentacles, use a range of media to draw, then colour, their version. Alternatively an image of a giant squid could be projected onto a whiteboard and children could draw the outline before colouring appropriately.
6	**Putting it together** • Can cut out their fish and other animals, and place them to make a coherent image. • Can work with others and reflect and discuss work.	• To reflect on what they and others have done and say what they think and feel about it and suggest ways in which they might change or develop their work • To work safely with a range of tools	Cut out the seahorses, fish and giant squid and place in the ocean background, considering relative depths. Add glitter or other decorations, as desired. Discuss the process together and reflect on the work, the decisions and the finished work with a partner, in a group or as a class.

Notes:
The unit also provides opportunities to explore the work of great artists describing differences and similarities, see' Background knowledge' section for suggestions.

Year 1 Background knowledge

Weather

Where possible introduce sessions with stimuli, including music, artists' work (see below), story, drama and dance so that children have the opportunity to discuss and experience different weather conditions prior to using materials for their interpretations.

Artists work can be found on many websites, including: www.bbc.co.uk/arts/yourpaintings/ and collections.vam.ac.uk/. Some examples to share with children: ***Sun and shadows**: Tall Shadows on the Park Wall* by John Atkinson Grimshaw and *Autumnal Woodland Scene* by John Noble Barlow.
Clouds: Constable, *Study of Clouds, Study of Cirrus, Study of Sky and trees*.
Autumn leaves: Find work by Andy Goldsworthy – search online for 'Andy Goldsworthy + leaves'. (**NB** You should check the terms of use of websites before sharing with children.)

Gardens

2Paint a Picture (published by 2Simple) is a very easy-to-use painting program for primary school children, which allows them to experiment with a variety of brush styles, make simple patterns and experiment with colour mixing.

The Paint and Colour programmes and video on the 'I am an artist' website (www.iamanartist.ie) offer opportunities to see and hear the children discussing colours and their reactions to mixing them. You can also hear the children discussing their paintings.

Bugs and beetles

Getting started in clay

- Provide each child with a clay mat. Let the group pass round a container of hand cream and rub a small dot into their hands. Cut each child two lumps of clay, about the size of a small orange, which they should wedge (knock into balls firmly with the heel of the hand, turning the clay after each knock, to burst any air bubbles which could cause the work to explode in the kiln).
- The children place one ball of clay on the mat between the two wooden guides (see Figure 1). Place the guides to allow room for the clay to expand when rolled.
- The children use the rollers to gradually roll the ball of clay flat until the roller rests on the guides. Teach them to roll away from the body – not to and fro – to encourage any remaining air bubbles to be forced out in one direction. (The principle is exactly the opposite of making pastry, where the cook tries to incorporate air into the dough.) The rolled ball of clay should end up in a natural oval shape. Discourage fingering the smooth surface! (From 'Turtle textures', *Child Education,* 27th May, 2008 by Jane Bower. Complete article available on www.scholastic.co.uk/childeducation)

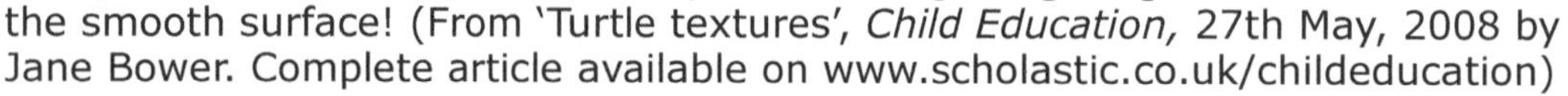

FIGURE 1

Session 4: Look at butterfly images, made in paper. Rebecca Coles' website has many fine examples: www.rebeccajcoles.co.uk.

Sessions 4 & 5: Display the butterflies and snails alongside digital photographs taken by children. If time permits, make and paint a clay giant sunflower, display together: consider the scale.

Fireworks

Children's experiences of fireworks can be enhanced by showing photographs and short video clips.

Relevant paintings containing fireworks or with firework compositions can be found on gallery websites and on the BBC 'Your Paintings' website – where you will find *Fireworks* by Ben Nicholson and *Fireworks at Queen's Festival* by Joseph McWilliams (NB check for terms of use).

Under the sea

Source images of fish and animals found under the sea, including seahorses and giant squid.

After completing the unit, two paintings on the BBC 'Your Paintings' website would make a good discussion point:
Still Life under the Sea (Mary Kessell, 1960)
Under the Sea (Polyptych; Members of the Rural Youth Project, 2008).

Year 2 Long-term planning

Aim 1: Exploring and creating

The National Curriculum states that children should be taught:
- to use a range of materials creatively to design and make products.
- to use drawing, painting and sculpture to… share their ideas, experiences and imagination.

Make and record observations first-hand and from memory.

Develop their ideas, try things out and ask questions.

Explore thoughts and ideas using their experience, imagination and originality through a range of creative opportunities.

Children experience and learn about:
- the art of Victorian times: portraits, cameos, still life and illustration
- printing with vegetables and fruit
- straight line and curvy sculpture
- art techniques using *Elmer* the elephant
- the art of Paul Klee
- seaside mosaics and creating a diorama.

Aim 2: Skills and techniques

The National Curriculum states that children should be taught:
- to develop… techniques in using colour, pattern, texture, line, shape, form and space.

To experience and develop techniques in drawing, painting, sculpture and collage with a variety of materials and tools including ICT, children develop their artistic techniques in:
- drawing from observation, memory and imagination
- using a digital camera to take photographs
- creating a silhouette cut-out and still-life collage
- painting using a range of media and combining different media
- a range of printing methods
- a range of different sculptures
- making a soft toy
- printing using stencils
- creating collage by combining a range of different materials and media
- using colour and working like an artist.

Work safely with a range of tools and techniques, including appropriate new technology tools, taking care of themselves and others.

Aim 3: Evaluate and analyse

The National Curriculum states that children should be taught:
- to use drawing, painting and sculpture to develop and share their ideas, experiences and imagination.

Reflect on what they and others have done and say what they think and feel about it.

Suggest ways in which they might change or develop their work.

Throughout the units of work children should be encouraged to record, annotate and modify their work as often as possible creating a personal source of information and ideas, including:
- talking about their work and how they achieved it
- developing an appropriate vocabulary
- trying out different ideas and designs
- identifying ways in which their work can be improved upon
- talk about and give opinions on the work of others.

Aim 4: Art and artists

The National Curriculum states that children should be taught:
- about the work of a range of artists, craft makers and designers, describing the differences and similarities between different practices and disciplines, and making links to their own work.

Learn about, understand and value the work of artists, craft makers and designers; the differences and similarities between them and making links to their own work.

Children learn about the works of a range of artists, including:
- Charles Dobson
- Henry Rousseau
- Wassily Kandinsky
- Piet Mondrian
- Barbara Hepworth
- Henry Moore
- Paul Klee.

Overview of progression in Year 2

Throughout the units in Year 2, children are:

- Making and recording observations first-hand, from memory and using their imagination.
- Explore and developing their ideas and experiences, using their imagination and originality through a range of creative opportunities.
- Learning about, understanding and valuing the work of artists, craft makers and designers; the differences and similarities between them and making links to their own works.
- Reflecting on what they and others have done and saying what they think and feel about it and suggesting ways in which they might change or develop their work.

Drawing

Through drawing Victorian portraits and illustrations, children are:

- Drawing on different surfaces and with a range of media.
- Experimenting to create different lines and marks made with a range of media.

Through studying *Elmer* and seaside art, children are:

- Drawing on different surfaces and with a range of media.

Painting

Through creating a series of Victorian portraits, children are:

- Using a variety of paint media and experimenting to produce a range of effects.
- Identifying primary colours and undertaking simple colour-mixing to include shades and tones.

Through exploring *Elmer* the elephant, children are:

- Using a variety of paint media and experimenting to produce a range of effects.
- Using a variety of tools and techniques including different brushes and investigating the kinds of marks which can be made.
- Identifying primary colours and undertaking simple colour-mixing to include shades and tones.

Through studying the art of Paul Klee, children are:

- Using a variety of paint media and experimenting to produce a range of effects.
- Identifying primary colours and undertaking simple colour-mixing to include shades and tones.
- Naming different types of paint and their properties.

Through painting pebbles in a seaside unit, children are:

- Using a variety of paint media and experimenting to produce a range of effects.
- Matching colours to artefacts and objects.

Printing

Through making their vegetable and fruit prints, children are:

- Using a range of found objects to make prints.
- Creating simple printing blocks using press printing techniques.
- Creating different simple designs by:
  - repeating patterns
  - overprinting.

Year 2 Complete 'Overview of progression' is provided on the CD-ROM, including 'Collage and textiles' and 'Sculpture' objectives.

Medium-term planning: 1. Victoriana

This unit of work offers a series of drawing and painting activities that encourage children to develop their skills and techniques around a common theme of Victoriana.

YEAR 2

W	Outcomes	Objectives	Skills and understanding
1	**Victorian portraits 1** • Can create a Victorian portrait from a photographic self-portrait.	• To experiment to create different lines and marks made with a range of media • To observe and identify key qualities and represent with line, colour and shade • To develop confidence in recording their first-hand observations • To explore the work of artists in different times and cultures	Show and discuss a range of Victorian portraits of children (see 'Background knowledge' for suggestions). Focus on key features of these portraits. Take digital portrait photograph of each child and print black and white copy. Children 'over paint' the photograph with ready-mix paints to create a Victorian-style self-portrait.
2	**Victorian portraits 2** • Can use various media to 'age' a photograph image to make a Victorian portrait.	• To experiment with media to create lighter and darker tones	Examine Victorian photographs and discuss colours. Use cameras take individual portraits (in Victorian costume if possible). Or use photographs from previous session. Print black and white copies. Use either weak cooled coffee (1 spoonful per cup) or watercolours to create the sepia image. Additional features can be added using brown paint.
3	**Cameo** • Can use experience to draw an outline, including strong detail.	• To use drawing technique to respond to what is seen • To develop confidence in their ability to draw things they observe and develop technique to represent them	Display some images of Victorian silhouettes and discuss how they were made. Create head silhouettes either by tracing a thick black outline of head onto white paper using a light source, or by tracing around the outline of a side-view photograph. Image is cut out and placed against a pastel background to create a cameo.
4	**Still life 1** • Can create a still-life composition by arranging cut-out pictures and photographs of objects.	• To observe and identify key qualities of natural and seen objects, represent lines and shapes • To cut shapes, from a variety of materials and arrange to create either an abstract or representational picture • To explore the work of artists in different times and cultures	Display some images of Victorian still life for discussion. Ensure children understand what is meant by a 'still-life' composition. From magazines, old calendars and photocopied prints, children cut out objects for their composition. These are then placed, discussed, then rearranged and glued on to a neutral background paper to make a still-life composition.
5	**Still life 2** • Can draw what is observed and create a still-life collage showing scale and overlap.	• To develop confidence in recording their first-hand observations • To use painting techniques to respond to what is seen, remembered or imagined	Children draw a still-life composition either using objects from the classroom, which they draw and add colour to using paints, pastels or pencils. Alternately, they use their still-life composition from the last session as a basis for their drawing.
6	**Charcoal illustration** • Can respond to observation and create illustration using appropriate effects.	• To observe and identify key qualities of seen objects, represent lines and shapes • To experiment to create different effects made with a range of media – different pencils and charcoal	Through observation and discussion of Dickensian illustrations, explore the line, shapes and shadows. Use drawing tools, pencils and charcoal, to firstly experiment with technique then move on to draw a building in a Dickensian style.

Notes:
Digital art: To create and manipulate digital portraits see *Art Express* Year 2, Unit 6 (Bloomsbury).

YEAR 2

Medium-term planning: 2. Vegetable and fruit printing

This unit of work offers a series of activities that introduce and develop a range of printing skills and techniques using fruit and vegetables.

W	Outcomes	Objectives	Skills and understanding
1	**Exploring vegetables** • Can experiment using different vegetables to make prints, and can identify the prints made.	• To use a range of found objects to make prints • To impress different textures and patterns • To talk about what they and others have made	Provide with a range of whole vegetables, paint to use as printing ink, mixing trays and sponges. Use whole vegetable as printing block, with either a single colour or pre-mixed colours. Discuss amount of paint required for print. Compare prints and identify vegetables used.
2	**Mushroom overprinting** • Can experiment using different paints to overprint an image.	• To explore patterns and pictures by printing with objects both natural and man-made • To create simple designs with repeating patterns	Cut mushrooms in half, to create a flat printing surface. Challenge children to create repeating patterns and to use different colours to over print the images, creating different effects and patterns.
3	**Citrus block printing 1** • Can create a simple block print from slices of fruit.	• To explore patterns and pictures by printing with objects both natural and man-made • To create simple printing blocks, use press printing techniques • To create simple designs with repeating patterns	This is an introduction to relief block printing. Cut oranges, lemons and limes into 0.5cm thick slices, with assistance. Glue slices to a square of thick cardboard to create a simple relief block. Using orange, yellow and green paint as the printing ink, create images and repeated patterns based on the citrus fruits.
4	**Citrus block printing 2** • Can create a simple relief block print using the impress method.	• To explore patterns and pictures by printing with objects both natural and man-made • To create simple printing blocks, use press printing techniques • To create simple designs with repeating patterns	Building on work in the previous session, create block for printing from a polystyrene square tile. Create a citrus fruit design on the polystyrene square tile using either a pencil or biro, pressing hard. Use the blocks, with paint as the ink, to create repeating patterns.
5	**Jungle prints 1** • Can use printing skills and techniques to create a jungle background.	• To explore patterns and pictures by printing with objects both natural and man-made • To create simple designs with repeating patterns and overprinting • To explore the work of artists in different times and cultures	Show examples of jungle paintings and pictures, such as Henry Rousseau. Provide a range of cut fruits and vegetables, paint to use as printing ink, mixing trays and sponges. Encourage children to use a range of prints, colours and shapes to produce a jungle background. Suggest experimenting with overprinting, and more complex repeating patterns.
6	**Jungle prints 2** • Can use stencil printing skills to add an animal foreground to complete a jungle composition.	• To explore patterns and pictures by printing with objects both natural and man-made – using both hard and soft materials • To create simple designs with repeating patterns and overprinting	Demonstrate how to print using a stencil and sponges. Using the jungle background from the previous session, overprint using a range of ready-made animal stencils to complete the print composition.

Notes:
Session 1: It is suggested that you use use whole vegetables in this session; however depending on the skill of the children cut vegetables can be used. Whole vegetables are more difficult to manipulate (and more messy!), whereas cut vegetables can make an easier introduction to the skills and techniques.

Medium-term planning: 3. Straight-line and curvy sculpture

This unit of work offers a series of activities that introduce and develop a range of sculpture skills and techniques, exploring different types of sculpture

W	Outcomes	Objectives	Skills and understanding
1	**Straight sculpture 1** • Can use experience and imagination to create a response using a range of media and paper.	• To use a range of tools safely when making models and sculptures • To use different construction materials creatively to make 3D models	Explore and discuss a range of straight sculptures; look at the edges and the lines. Collect cereal boxes (one for each child), deconstruct and flatten. Look at the shape of the box, in particular any tabs and slots; additional tabs and slots can be added. Cover the inside of the box with white paint using large brushes.
2	**Straight sculpture 2** • Can use paint and colour mixing to paint sculpture in an abstract way.	• To use painting tools and techniques to respond in the desired style • To experiment freely with paint and tools • To explore the work of artists in different times and cultures and make links to their own work	Explore the abstract shapes used by Kandinsky and Mondrian; take note of the angular lines and geometric shapes. Using an agreed range of colours – important for the final construction – add angular marks and geometric shapes to the painted box. Experiment with different brushes and other tools. When dry the box is re-constructed with the painted surfaces now forming the outside of the box.
3	**Assemble** • Can use skills to join materials to create a sculptural effect.	• To use simple techniques to join materials and make 3D constructions • To cooperate with other children	Begin the sculpture (can be a whole class or group assembly) by forming a stable base constructed from a few large, interlocked sections. When the base is in place, experiment with slotting different boxes in different positions, then fix in position.
4	**Barbara's garden** • Can respond to a range of sculptures to create a 3D sculpture from malleable materials.	• To manipulate malleable materials in a variety of ways to produce imaginative creations • To investigate different joining techniques • To explore the work of artists in different times and cultures and make links to their own work	Explore Barbara Hepworth's Garden (see below). Discuss the curves, the holes and the texture of the sculpture. Roll an even slab of clay that is then cut and shaped to form several pieces of flat clay. Cut out geometrical shapes from pieces before joining pieces together to form a 3D sculpture.
5	**Henry Moore** • Can use paint and colour mixing and a range of painting tools to finish a sculpture.	• To manipulate malleable materials in a variety of ways to produce imaginative creations	Show a range of large sculptures by Henry Moore. Provide each child with a large lump of clay which they shape into an organic sculpture by pulling, pinching and creating holes. Using slip, children smooth their final sculpture before leaving to dry.
6	**Varnish** • Can use paint and colour mixing and a range of painting tools to decorate a sculpture.	• To experiment with a range of brush sizes to create patterns in paint • To know about simple colour mixing	Use ready-mix paint to decorate sculptures, displaying wavy organic patterns created by using a range of brushes and other tools and interesting colour mixes. When dry, PVA glue is used to varnish the finished sculpture.

Notes:
Barbara Hepworth's Garden (http://kids.tate.org.uk/games/barbaras_garden) is an interactive resource that allows children to explore sculptures in the garden of the studio formerly used by the sculptor, now part of the Tate Gallery in St Ives, Cornwall.

Medium-term planning: 4. *Elmer* the elephant

This unit of work develops a range of painting, printing and textiles skills and techniques around a common theme of the popular children's book, *Elmer*.

W	Outcomes	Objectives	Skills and understanding
1	**My *Elmer*** • Can use colours to create own version of *Elmer*, using painting and problem solving techniques.	• To experiment freely with paint, to learn how to use it • To start to develop an appropriate vocabulary to describe and compare colours • To identify primary colours by name	Display *Elmer* and talk about the colours used to create the pattern. Using the 'My Elephant' template, use six primary and secondary colours to paint Elmer, making sure that no two colours are adjacent. Encourage discussion of the problem-solving element of the painting.
2	**Elmer make-over** • Can use a variety of tools to create different marks as part of a pattern.	• To experiment with tools – layering, mixing media, scraping through	Again use the 'My Elephant' template, with squares, but this time create a patterned *Elmer* making full use of a range of drawing tools to create different marks and patterns in the squares. When the patterned squares are completed, add colour using pencils, crayons or felt-tipped pens.
3	***Elmer* toy 1** • Can safely cut out template shape from felt or other material and stitch together.	• To cut shapes, from a variety of materials • To know and talk about different types, colours and textures of fabrics • To use simple stitches to join materials	Provide a range of patterned and plain fabrics, including felt, which can be used to make a stuffed toy and an enlarged 'My Elephant' template to aid cutting. After cutting two 'sides', use a range of decorating products which could be stitched or glued on – sequins, fringing, beads, glitter, paper boarders and ribbons.
4	***Elmer* toy 2** • Can use imagination to add decoration, showing a range of stitching and gluing techniques.	• To know and talk about different types, colours and textures of fabrics • To use simple stitches to join and decorate materials	Finish any outstanding decorations. Then blanket stitch together the two sides leaving a large gap unstitched. Add stuffing before completing stitching.
5	***Elmer* stencil print** • Can create a sponge print using a stencil.	• To make patterns and pictures by printing with objects both natural and man-made • To use stencils and sponge printing to create repeated images • To use a range of decorative techniques	From strong card, prepare a cut-out elephant outline and an elephant stencil. Using a range of ready-mix paints, sponge print around the outline and sponge print using the stencil. This will create negative and positive prints of *Elmer*. When dry, use a range of decorative materials and pens to add decoration and finish to *Elmer*.
6	**Stained glass *Elmer*** • Can use experience and imagination to create a response using a range of media and paper.	• To use painting tools and techniques to respond to what is seen, remembered or imagined • To know how to combine different media	Show examples of stained glass windows. Use black wax crayons to draw a stained glass version of Elmer (provide template to be drawn over). Each square of *Elmer* is decorated using different patterns and swirls using a range of wax crayons. Finally, the drawing is painted over using a range of watercolour paints.

Notes:
The original *Elmer* and subsequent *Elmer* titles are written by David McKee. There is currently a useful interview with David McKee on YouTube about the creation of Elmer. A 'My Elephant' template is available on the CD-ROM for the activities above.

Medium-term planning: 5. Paul Klee

This unit of work gives children the opportunity to learn about and experiment with colours and colour-mixing using the abstract works of Paul Klee as a stimulus.

W	Outcomes	Objectives	Skills and understanding
1	**Primary colours** • Can name and mix primary and secondary colours.	• To use painting techniques to respond to what is seen, remembered or imagined • To mix and match a range of primary and secondary colours • To explore the work of artists in different times and cultures	Explain that red, yellow and blue are called primary colours and that when two primary colours are mixed they create a secondary colour. Opportunity to mix and ready-mix paint blocks of different primary and secondary colours on a blank canvas.
2	**Secondary colours** • Can name and mix primary and secondary colours.	• To use painting techniques to respond to what is seen, remembered or imagined • To mix and match a range of primary and secondary colours • To explore the work of artists in different times and cultures	**Focus work: *Castle and Sun*** Show work by Paul Klee as an example of abstract art – what parts of the painting can be identified. Create own version of *Castle and Sun* by mixing and applying primary and secondary colours using ready-mix paints.
3	**Mixing greens** • Can consolidate knowledge of mixing a range of green colours.	• To use painting techniques to respond to what is seen, remembered or imagined • To know how to combine different media • To mix and match a range of primary and secondary colours	This lesson consolidates secondary colour mixing of green by mixing blue and yellow. **Focus work: *Around the Fish*** Focus attention on the fish and the pattern scales. Introduce wax resist technique using blue and green crayons to draw fish and large scales. Scales and rest of fish painted using a range of green, blues and yellows.
4	**Mixing purples** • Can consolidate knowledge of mixing a range of purple colours.	• To use painting techniques to respond to what is seen, remembered or imagined • To know how to combine different media • To mix and match a range of primary and secondary colours	This lesson consolidates secondary colour mixing of purple by mixing blue and red. **Focus work: *Fire in the Evening*** Use laminated squares and rectangles that are drawn around to create an abstract drawing in the style of the painting. Blocks of a range of reds, blues and purples are added using a watercolour paints.
5	**Mixing oranges** • Can consolidate knowledge of mixing a range of orange colours.	• To use painting techniques to respond to what is seen, remembered or imagined • To know how to combine different media • To mix and match a range of primary and secondary colours	This lesson consolidates secondary colour mixing of orange by mixing red and yellow. **Focus work: *Senecio*** A simple self-portrait is drawn in pencil in the style of the painting. Colour is added using chalk pastels that are mixed together to create a range of yellows, reds and oranges.
6	**Paul Klee letters** • Can create a composition in the style of Paul Klee.	• To use painting techniques to respond to what is seen, remembered or imagined • To know how to combine different media • To mix and match a range of primary and secondary colours	**Focus work: *Letters*** Use a theme to encourage a number of words that are written using a simple 'ball and stick' handwriting style on pre-drawn lines on sugar paper. Suggested medium is charcoal for writing. Blocks of colour are added using a range of media: • ready-mix • watercolours • chalk pastels

Notes:
At the end of each session make links between the work of Paul Klee and the children's own work.
The Scholastic website includes a number of articles and activities about the work of Paul Klee. In particular, the activity sheet 'Create a brochure collage inspired by Paul Klee' would be useful for this unit (Visit www.scholastic.co.uk/100artanddesign).
Digital art: All of these lessons could be adapted for using a paint software package.
In session 6, possible themes to encourage words for the composition are 'my favourite things', 'my family', 'my friends at school'.

YEAR 2

Medium-term planning: 6. At the seaside

This unit of work offers a series of activities that introduce and develop a range of different skills and techniques around a common theme of the seaside culminating in a seascape diorama.

W	Outcomes	Objectives	Skills and understanding
1	**Paper sculpture** • Can create a free standing paper sculpture.	• To create sculpture using paper modelling and construction, joining recycled, natural and man-made materials	Using thick white card create a free-standing paper sculpture of a fish. Decorate the fish using paints and prints, if desired, then choose from a range of decorative art materials (glitter, beads etc.). The base of the sculpture is hidden using 'wave crests', on both sides of the fish, made of green, blue and white strips of sugar paper curled around a pencil.
2	**Sand sculpture** • Can use imagination to create a sculpture in sand.	• To explore sculpture with a range of malleable materials	Use dampened play sand in a large tray. Using a range of tools to sculpt and plastic bowls and beakers as moulds, create a sandcastle sculpture. Finished sculpture can be decorated using a range of materials including found objects such as shells and stones, flags and other art materials. Photograph sculpture for class display.
3	**Seaside mosaic** • Can create a mosaic using paper collage techniques.	• To sort and group materials for different purposes • To arrange and glue materials to different backgrounds	Show a range of photographs and pictures depicting things normally associated with the seaside (crabs, starfish, ice cream). Choose an image and draw it onto a large sheet of paper. Show examples of mosaic tile pictures. Drawings are then completed in the mosaic style using ready-made paper squares.
4	**Sun and clouds** • Can use a range of materials to make collage sun and clouds.	• To cut out shapes, from a variety of materials and arrange to create either an abstract or representational picture	Use paper plates, paint and tissue paper to make a summer sun for display; embellishing it with glitter and tissue paper to depict its rays. Cut cloud shapes (encourage imagination) from white cardboard, adding cotton wools to finish.
5	**Pebbles** • Can use appropriate painting technique to paint pebbles for seaside collage.	• To mix and match colours to artefacts and objects	Select appropriate pebbles and small stones to decorate for a seaside display or collage. Encourage discussion about the process of 'making ready' then painting the pebbles, and about the type of image which would work best in the display or collage.
6	**Seascape** • Can use a range of art techniques to create a diorama.	• To arrange and glue materials to different backgrounds • To use a range of paint media to create a range of effects • To draw on different surfaces using a range of media	Children use a range of techniques to create a mixed media diorama: • Background of the sun and sunset made of mosaic tiles (see lesson 3) • Sea and waves swirls and patterns are drawn on to white card and then added as the foreground of the diorama. • Children draw and paint a yacht which is used for the middle part of the diorama. Add other items as part of display.

Notes:
A number of these sessions could be extended to discuss scientific concepts associated with the sun and clouds (session 4) and rocks (session 5).

Year 2 Background knowledge

Victoriana

Introduce sessions with stimuli, including music, artists' work (see below), story, drama etc.

One Victorian artist who has many paintings including Victorian children is William Dobson. Two recommended paintings are: *A bowl of cherries* and *A Venetian girl*, on BBC Your Paintings website.

Session 3: View 'Victorian silhouettes' on the web; check images first, there are some which are not appropriate!

Note: Original cameo brooches have a dark background and a white, or cream, silhouette. To create this effect, draw and cut out the oval, as before. Draw the face, leaving it white while colouring in the remainder of the oval – the background – black.

Sessions 4, 5 & 6: Victorian still-life paintings are to be found on the BBC 'Your Paintings' website, or on the web; Dickensian illustrations are also to be found online. (**NB** You should check the terms of use of websites before sharing with children.)

Vegetable printing (prints)

Whole vegetables for printing might include: broccoli, corn, carrots, cabbage, cauliflower.

Cut fruit and vegetables for printing might include: broccoli, onion, celery, mushrooms, leek, courgette, star fruit, kiwi fruit, apple, oranges and lemons.

Cut fruit in different ways – lengthwise and crosswise. Think of other options, e.g. horizontal cut into an apple to show the interior star shape, or create rosette, crescent moons, fish scales and more from celery.

Cut as flat as possible to provide an even printing surface. (It may take a few attempts before the stamp is appropriately saturated.) When printing using an onion, use a fork as a handle to keep hands away from the onion, because it can be slippery to hold.

If cutting fruit, use adult support or only allow children to use plastic cutting implements.

If using tempura paint, add a little liquid soap to each colour; have each colour in a different tray. Also supply trays for mixing colours and a damp sponge by each tray.

Session 2: Can be completed using other cut vegetables such as celery (see above) or fruit.

Sessions 5 & 6: Henri Rousseau images are available online.
The National Gallery have a children's interactive 'jungle' game: www.nga.gov/kids/zone/jungle.

Straight-line and curvy sculptures

There are many sculpture images available via search engines, or from the websites of galleries such as the Tate. The BBC has an archive interview, done for *Blue Peter*, with Henry Moore available online. In addition these websites might prove useful:
www.barbarahepworth.org.uk; www.henry-moore.org; http://sculpture.uk.com

Different types of clay

Modelling or earthenware clays: If possible give children the opportunity to handle natural clays as they are more pleasant to touch. If you do not have access to a kiln, sculptures can be dried slowly, painted, and varnished (two coats) to strengthen.
Red clay: This is reddish brown in its natural state; it gets its colour from the iron it contains. It may stain hands and equipment.
Grey or white clay: This is usually referred to in catalogues as 'buff' or 'ivory', as this is the colour it becomes when fired. It is easy to use and is kinder on the hands. When it is dry it provides a lighter base on which to paint.
Self-hardening clay: This clay can contain fibres and is less brittle when dry. This means fairly durable clay work can be produced without firing. However, it is more expensive than natural clay; some dislike the 'feel' and believe children should be offered 'the real thing'.
Cold clay: A natural clay with hardener. It can be used like ordinary clay but does not need to be fired.

Paul Klee

Paul Klee was a Swiss painter who is regarded as one of the founders of Modern Art. Images of his work are available from the Tate Gallery website or from www.paulklee.net.

Works which could be used as a stimulus include:
- *Castle and Sun*
- *Around the Fish*
- *Fire in the Evening*
- *Senecio*

Year 3 Long-term planning

Aim 1: Exploring and creating

The National Curriculum states that children should be taught... with creativity, experimentation and an increasing awareness of different kinds of art, craft and design:
- to create sketch books to record their observations.

Select and record from first-hand observation and experience.

Use their imagination and originality to explore ideas for different purposes.

Record, annotate and modify work in their sketchbooks by:
- recording from observation, memory and their imagination
- trying out and evaluate their ideas
- designing for a range of different ideas and products.

Children experience and learn about:
- the art of Vincent Van Gogh
- techniques in printing
- creating 2D and 3D sculptures in clay
- a range of Celtic Crafts.

Aim 2: Skills and techniques

The National Curriculum states that children should be taught:
- to develop their techniques, including their control and their use of materials.
- to improve their mastery of art and design techniques, including drawing, painting and sculpture with a range of materials.

To improve their mastery of techniques such as drawing, painting, sculpture and collage with materials such as pencil, charcoal, paint, clay, textiles and ICT.

Children develop their artistic techniques in:
- drawing from observation, memory and their imagination
- drawing lines, shapes and figures with increasing accuracy and detail
- using a digital camera to take photographs
- frottage – making wax rubbings of textures
- painting using a range of media and combining different media
- making a soft toy
- a range of printing methods
- creating a clay bas relief sculpture
- making ceramic pots
- batik to add designs to a cloth
- collage
- weaving.

Aim 3: Evaluate and analyse

The National Curriculum states that children should be taught:
- to create sketch books to record their observations and them to review and revisit ideas.

Reflect on their own and others' work, comparing ideas and methods and adapting their work accordingly.

Describe how their work might develop further.

Throughout the units of work children should be encouraged to record, annotate and modify their work at all stages of the creative process creating a personal source of information and ideas, including:
- trying out different ideas and designs in their sketchbooks and identifying ways in which their work can be improved upon
- deciding on the best design *from their sketchbook* and using this to inform future work
- using their sketchbook to record *their own work and to include* ideas and work of other artists (this can include photographs, pictures of other works of art, examples of different media and techniques)
- use their sketchbooks to experiment with using different media and practising different skills and techniques.

Aim 4: Art and artists

The National Curriculum states that children should be taught:
- about the greatest artists, architects and designers in history.

Explore the work of artists, craft makers, and designers working in different times and cultures, including examples selected for them to view and through visits to museums and galleries and online collections.

Children learn about the works of a range of artists, including:
- Vincent Van Gogh
- Rebecca Coles
- Maurice Sendak
- Celtic craft makers.

Overview of progression in Year 3

Throughout the units in Year 3, children are:

- Using sketchbooks to collect and record visual information and ideas from different sources.
- Working from a variety of sources including observation, photographs and digital images.

Drawing

Through drawing buildings in the locality, children are:

- Developing close observation skills, including using view finders.
- Making marks and lines with a wide range of drawing implements including graphite pencils (5B–5H).
- Using different grades of pencil and other implements to create lines, draw different shapes and forms and to produce variations in tone.
- Exploring ways in which surface detail can be added to drawings through applying different patterns and textures, including shading and hatching.

Through drawing different 'wild things' children are:

- Making marks and lines with a wide range of drawing implements including graphite pencils and fine line pens.
- Using different grades of pencil and other implements to create lines, draw different shapes and forms and to produce variations in tone.

Painting

Through learning about, and painting in the style of Van Gogh, children are:

- Creating imaginative work from a variety of sources e.g. observational drawing, themes, inspirational works of art.
- Creating different effects and textures using a range of techniques and paints.
- Extending knowledge of colour theory, in particular tints, tones and shades.
- Using colour to create atmosphere and to show the effect of light.
- Developing an awareness of composition, scale and proportion in their paintings.

Printing

Through experiencing a range of print workshops based on butterflies, children are:

- Creating printing blocks using a relief or impressed method.
- Using initial sketchbook ideas to create motifs that are made into printing blocks and stencils.
- Creating different printing effects by using repeating patterns and block rotation.

Collage and textiles

Through a range of Celtic craft activities, children are:

- Experiencing a range of textile techniques such as weaving to create different textural effects.

Through learning about Van Gogh, children are:

- Experiencing a range of textile techniques such as batik to create textural effects.

By making a soft toy based on an animal from the Savannah, children are:

- Creating 3D structures from different textiles.
- Developing skills in using tools to manipulate textiles through stitching, cutting, joining.
- Applying a range of decorative finishes to provide detail and to enhance the textile.

Year 3 Complete 'Overview of progression' is provided on the CD-ROM, including 'Sculpture' objectives.

Medium-term planning: 1. Down our street

YEAR 3

This unit of work focuses on creating images of buildings in the streets around the school. These images are made using a range of media, including pencil, pen, crayon and clay.

W	Outcomes	Objectives	Skills and understanding
1 2	**Images from the locality** • Can make observational drawings of buildings. • Can use viewfinders to locate features of local buildings. • Can use a digital camera to take photographs of buildings and parts of buildings. • Can create frottage by making wax rubbings of different surface textures of buildings.	• To develop greater control and confidence in using a range of drawing tools and media • To respond to what is observed or remembered through drawing • To know that making a print involves transferring an image from one surface to another	Using building close to school, facilitate workshops on: - Observational drawing - Photography - Frottage For observational drawings focus on whole buildings (colour with watercolours) and then use viewfinders to focus on certain aspects – doors, windows, brickwork, patterns and shapes. Taking digital photographs of building and features of buildings (as above). Make a series of wax rubbings of surfaces of buildings.
3	**Building collage** • Can make a collage picture of a building by combining a range of media.	• To combine a range of materials to create a collage • To represent natural or man-made objects using collage materials	Using a range of images from the previous sessions, create a collage of local buildings by combining drawings, photographs and frottage.
4	**Creating a clay bas relief** • Can experiment with different designs, patterns and textures on a clay slab. • Can join pieces of clay to a slab of clay to create a clay bas relief.	• To design and make for a particular purpose • To understand the importance of using tools appropriately and safely • To manipulate malleable materials to make 2D compositions • To blend and join surfaces of malleable materials • To apply a range of patterns, textures and decorative finishes to malleable materials	Create a flat slab of clay by rolling a ball of clay between guide sticks to create an even, flat slab. Use clay modelling tools to create patterns and designs on a slab of clay. Experiment with adding pieces of clay to the slab to create an abstract design using the scratch and slip method. When dry, abstract designs can be sprayed with metallic paint.
5	**Building sculpture 1** • Can create a clay bas relief sculpture based on a drawing of a building in the locality.	• To understand the importance of using tools appropriately and safely • To manipulate malleable materials to make 2D compositions • To blend and join surfaces of malleable materials	Using a sketchbook drawing of a building (from earlier session), create a clay bas relief sculpture of a local building. Shape and cut the clay slab to form the basic shape of the building and use a range of tools to create a textured surface with patterns. Create additional features from clay and use scratch and slip method to join them to the slab to create the relief sculpture.
6	**Building sculpture 2** • Can mix and match colours to match those from observational drawings of a building in the locality. • Can accurately apply colours to a clay bas relief.	• To apply a range of patterns, textures and decorative finishes to malleable materials	Using sketches from earlier sessions as a guide, mix and apply a range of colours to the clay bas relief. Apply a coat of varnish to complete the relief sculpture.

Notes:

Digital art: There is an opportunity during this unit to create a digital montage of local buildings using software such as Photoshop. Scan the drawings and add them to the software package to create a montage of images.

Medium-term planning: 2. Butterflies

This unit of work offers a series of activities that introduce and develop a range of printing skills and techniques around a common theme of butterflies.

W	Outcomes	Objectives	Skills and understanding
1	**Butterfly wings** • Can make a detailed study on the shape and colour of different butterfly wings.	• To develop greater control and confidence in using a range of drawing tools and media • To respond to what is observed or remembered through drawing	Provide a range of images of butterflies. Use viewfinders to focus on patterns and colours. Sketchbooks: focus on shape of the wings. Draw and colour the shape and the patterns on the wings.
2	**Mono-printing** • Can create a mono-print of a butterfly focusing on shape and pattern of the wings.	• To know that making a print involves transferring an image from one surface to another • To understand and apply a range of printmaking processes – mono-printing	An image is made on a whiteboard using paint and fine brushes. A print is made by pressing down a piece of paper.
3	**Relief printing block** • Can create a printing block using a simple relief method. • Can create different print patterns using a relief printing block.	• To know that making a print involves transferring an image from one surface to another • To know that the printing process can result in repeated images • To understand and apply a range of printmaking processes – relief printing	Draw a butterfly design on a square of thick cardboard. Completely cover the cardboard with PVA glue – allow getting sticky. Add elastic from elastic bands to create the drawn design. Leave to dry Experiment with different designs by repeating the pattern, overlaying or rotating the print block.
4	**Impress printing block** • Can draw an intricate design on polystyrene to create an impress block print. • Can create simple repeating patterns of butterflies.	• To know that making a print involves transferring an image from one surface to another • To know that the printing process can result in repeated images • To understand and apply a range of printmaking processes – impress printing	Draw intricate butterfly designs in a sketchbook then select the best to transfer to a square of polystyrene. Use ballpoint pen to create deep impression of the design. Apply paint or ink to printing block using either a sponge or a printing roller. Experiment with repeating designs and collaborating with other children to create repeated designs.
5	**Stencil printing** • Can create patterns of butterflies using stencil printing.	• To know that making a print involves transferring an image from one surface to another • To know that the printing process can result in repeated images	Create a symmetrical butterfly stencil by folding card and drawing then cutting out a design. Use sponges to apply paint to the stencil to create butterfly shapes. Experiment with mixing different colours. This can be extended to use ink diffusers as another way of adding colour to the stencil.
6	**Final composition: creating a large scale composition – 'The Butterfly Garden'** • Can combine a range of printing techniques to create a composition containing a number of butterflies.	• To understand and apply a range of printmaking processes • To understand the effect of combining different media	Create a simple background of green patterns to represent the garden. Use printing blocks and stencils from previous sessions to create butterfly images on a painted background. When dry use a range of art materials (sequins, glitter pens etc.) to add finishes and enhance the butterfly patterns.

Notes:
For all the printing activities it is recommended that the printing medium used is poster or acrylic paint.

YEAR 3

Medium-term planning: 3. Van Gogh

This unit of work is based around two of Van Gogh's most famous paintings. It provides an opportunity for mixed media composition as well as introducing the technique of batik.

W	Outcomes	Objectives	Skills and understanding
1	**Featured painting: *Starry Night over the Rhone*** • Can combine wax crayons and watercolour to produce a wax resist painting in the style of Van Gogh.	• To respond to imagination through painting • To understand the qualities and effects of a range of painting media • To learn about the work of artists from different times and cultures • To develop an awareness of how paintings are created • To explore the work of artists in different times and cultures	Display a range of works by Vincent Van Gogh and discuss with the class. Divide paper in half horizontally using a wax crayon line. Features such as buildings, windows, stars and street lamps are added above the line using yellow and white wax crayons. Paper is folded in half and vigorously rubbed to create a full page image. Blue colour washes are added to the drawing to create the wax resist painting.
2	**Featured painting: *The Starry Night*** • Can mix a range of blue colours using blue, black and white. • Can apply a range of colours to create a landscape background.	(As session 1)	Introduce the painting and discuss and establish its content. Using poster paints, experiment with mixing brilliant blue with black and white to produce a range of blue colours. Create own background painting with sky, hills and buildings using a range of blues.
3	**Featured painting: *The Starry Night*** • Can apply chalk pastels to create details in the style of *The Starry Night* by Van Gogh.	• To understand the effect of combining different media • To develop an awareness of how paintings are created	Using the painting from previous session: • use white and yellow pastels to create moon and stars and swirl patterns • use black pastel to enhance the building shapes and add fine detail to the painting.
4	**Starry night batik** • Can create a batik cloth in the style of Van Gogh's Starry Night.	• To decorate fabrics in a number of different ways and finishes • To use dyes, paints, batik, appliqué, etc. to make a textile design	Learn about the technique of batik. (Due to age of children, replace hot wax with PVA glue dispensed from a bottle.) Create a design of stars, moons and swirls using PVA glue on cotton cloth. When dry, paint with fabric paints in a range of blue colours and leave to dry. Soak cloth in warm water to soften the glue and then peel off leaving the design.
5	**Starry swirls** • Can create swirling prints using the technique of marbling.	• To know that making a print involves transferring an image from one surface to another • To understand and apply a range of printmaking processes – marbling	Review the method of creating patterned paper using marbling technique. Use as large a tray as possible to produce large scale marbled paper using blue, black and purple marbling ink. Use combs to create swirls in water before applying large sheets of paper.
6	**Final composition: My Starry Night** • Can use a range of media and techniques learnt in the session to create an original composition	• To understand the effect of combining different media • To use sketching to plan a composition • To use painting techniques for different purposes	The marbled paper from last session is used as the background for the composition. Decide on the different techniques and media to be used to create the composition elements, gather resources and plan the series of creative steps required. Create all the elements for the composition, which could be a group composition.

Notes:
Digital art: As an alternative to a marbled background, use a paint package to create a swirling background of stars.

Medium-term planning: 4. Savannah

This unit of work is based around animals found on the African Savannah. It provides opportunities to extend and consolidate skills in drawing, painting and sewing.

YEAR 3

W	Outcomes	Objectives	Skills and understanding
1	**Elephants** • Can draw an outline of an elephant. • Can design a multi-coloured elephant.	• To develop greater control and confidence in using a range of drawing tools and media • To respond to what is observed or remembered through drawing • To use sketching to plan a composition	Learn how to draw simple animals by combining a 'stick skeleton' with drawing ovals for the body shape. Study of side view of elephant photographs. Sketchbooks: • Sketch simple skeleton • Add ovals for body, head • Draw legs and trunk • Finish with large ears • When complete, decorate elephant outline in a 'fancy design'.
2	**Savannah scene 1** • Can draw outlines of several African animals.	• To develop greater control and confidence in using a range of drawing tools and media • To respond to what is observed or remembered through drawing • To use sketching to plan a composition	Provide a range of side view photographs of African wild animals. Sketchbooks: Using skills taught in previous session, sketch several animal outlines to form the basis of an African Savannah. Complete sketch with simple trees and grass.
3	**Savannah scene 2** • Can add colour to the composition by 'blocking in colours'.	• To respond to imagination through painting • To use sketching to plan a composition • To use painting techniques for different purposes	This session introduces the technique of blocking in colour using the Savannah sketch from the previous session. Demonstrate how to completely fill a shape with paint: • Loading the brush with paint • Painting sides of shape and manipulating brush head to create a line of paint. • Filling in the centre of the shape. Apply this technique to sketched composition starting with the lightest colours first.
4	**Designing and cutting** • Can create a fabric pattern by drawing a large outline of an animal. • Can cut out as pattern accurately using fabric scissors.	• To draw and cut out a fabric pattern	Choose animal design from sketchbook to turn into a stuffed toy. Draw large outline of animal on to paper that will act as the pattern for the fabric. Photocopy to create identical pattern. Pin pattern to sheets of felt and then cut out pattern to make pieces of the stuffed toy.
5	**Decorating** • Can use a range of stitching to decorate an animal pattern.	• To decorate fabrics in a number of different ways and finishes • To apply a range of sewing techniques and stitches to combine and decorate fabrics	Add additional fabric features such as ears to the cut-out pieces of felt. Decorate each part of the pattern using decorative stitches, buttons, beads etc.
6	**Sewing and finishing** • Can use blanket stitch to join pieces of fabric to create a stuffed animal. • Can add stuffing to create a soft toy.	• To apply a range of sewing techniques and stitches to combine and decorate fabrics	Join pieces of cloth (reversed) using a simple blanket stitch leaving a small gap for the stuffing to be inserted. Reverse the 'inside out' pattern and then stuff with filling ensuring that all areas are filled and equally stuffed. Finish off with blanket stitch to seal in the stuffing.

Notes:
Session 1: search 'Elephant parade + London' to view a range of painted elephants from recent initiatives.

Medium-term planning: 5. Celtic crafts

This unit of work is a series of craft activities that are taught through a cross-curricular topic of the Celts.

W	Outcomes	Objectives	Skills and understanding
1	**Celtic crosses** • Can design a Celtic cross from studying photographs and drawings of original designs. • Can create a Celtic cross sculpture by combining cardboard cut-outs.	• To create 3D objects from 2D materials • To design and make for a particular purpose • To use a range of adhesive and joining techniques when creating sculpture • To create a range of decorative finishes	Provide a range of images of Celtic crosses which are used as a stimulus to create an original design in sketchbooks. Following sketchbook designs, shapes are cut out from thick cardboard then assembled and joined together to form a Celtic cross.
2	**Celtic torcs** • Can create a Celtic torc using a malleable material such as clay or Plasticine®.	• To design and make for a particular purpose • To manipulate malleable materials to make 3D sculpture and objects • To blend and join surfaces of malleable materials • To apply a range of patterns, textures and decorative finishes to malleable materials	Provide a range of images of Celtic torcs. Demonstrate how to roll and then plait malleable material. Add additional design pieces using scratch and slip method. Use tools to add texture and patterns. When dry, torcs are sprayed with gold or silver paint.
3	**Ceramic coil pot** • Can create a simple ceramic pot using coiling method.	• To design and make for a particular purpose • To manipulate malleable materials to make 3D sculpture and objects • To blend and join surfaces of malleable materials	Demonstrate how to: • Roll clay into long lengths. • Create a simple base for the pot by coiling lengths of clay. • Building up the sides of the pot using coils. • Smoothing edges to join the coils together (inside and outside). Extension: Children make a lid for the pot or add handles using the scratch and slip method.
4	**An introduction to weaving** • Can create a simple weave from paper. • Understand the process and vocabulary of weaving.	• To make simple weaving looms and practise weaving skills	Understand that weaving is a process of forming cloth through interlacing yarn or thread. Children create a simple loom and warp threads by cutting vertical lines on folded sugar paper. They then thread the weft through the warp to create a weave. Extension: Children create the loom and warp using wavy or ziz-zag lines.
5	**Making a weaving loom** • Can create a simple loom frame from lolly sticks. • Can create warp threads by stringing vertical lengths of string.	• To make simple weaving looms and practise weaving skills	Following a demonstration, children create a simple frame by gluing four lolly sticks to make a square frame. Create vertical threads by wrapping string tightly to make the warp. Secure the warp with glue.
6	**Making the weave** • Can make a weave by threading the weft through the warp on a simple loom.	• To make simple weaving looms and practise weaving skills	The weft thread is attached to a large needle of paper clip acting as the shuttle. The weft thread is fed over and under the vertical warp threads to create the weave.

Notes:
While this unit of work is based around the history topic of 'The Celts' the activities can be modified to fit in with most British and ancient history topics in the new National Curriculum 2014.

Medium-term planning: 6. Wild things

This drawing, painting and sculpture unit is based on the book *Where the Wild Things Are*, by Maurice Sendak

W	Outcomes	Objectives	Skills and understanding
1	**Zig-zag drawing** • Can draw, with detail, different animal body parts. • Can use fine drawing skills to draw patterns and textures.	• To develop greater control and confidence in using a range of drawing tools and media • To respond to imagination through drawing	Traditional drawing game using black felt-tipped pens. After each body part has been drawn and obscured by folding, the drawing is swapped with a different child each time. • At the top of a piece of A4 paper, draw the head of an animal – remind children to draw eyes, ears, mouth/beak. • Next, draw a neck – add pattern. • Next draw the body – add features such as fur, feathers, scales or wings. • Next draw the legs – two or four? The drawing is returned to original owner to add colour to the complete drawing.
2	**Animal dice game** • Can draw, with detail, different animal body parts. • Can use fine drawing skills to draw patterns and textures.	• To develop greater control and confidence in using a range of drawing tools and media • To respond to imagination through drawing	Play the animal dice game in which the throw of a dice dictates the types of body parts each animal will have. Children copy from the game sheet the body parts to create their own animal and add additional features and then colours using pencils, felt-tipped pens or water colours.
3	**Collage of animals** • Can create a paper collage by combining cut-out pictures, photographs and drawings.	• To combine a range of materials to create a collage • To represent natural or man-made objects using collage materials	Combine a range of cut-out images of different animal body parts to create their fantasy animal collage. Accurately cut out animal images from newspapers, magazines, copies of books etc. and then cut the image into smaller body parts. These are then reassembled using different animal body parts to create new animals.
4	**Pinch pot elephant** • Can create simple body shape out of clay using pinch-pot technique. • Can model additional features in clay to join to the pinch pot.	• To manipulate malleable materials to make 3D sculpture and objects • To blend and join surfaces of malleable materials	In this demonstration session the teacher models and instructs each stage of the creative process. Use pinch-pot method to create an animal body in clay. Show scratch and slip method to attached additional features such as trunk, feet, ears and tail.
5	**Pinch pot beasts 1** • Can model additional features in clay to join to the pinch pot. • Can use modelling tools to add detail and pattern to the pinch pot beast.	• To manipulate malleable materials to make 3D sculpture and objects • To blend and join surfaces of malleable materials • To apply a range of patterns, textures and decorative finishes to malleable materials	Encourage children to use their imagination to envision and create their 'Wild Thing'. Use pinch-pot method to create main body from clay. Use scratch and slip method to attached additional features such as face, hands, feet, horns and tails. Use clay modelling tools to give the creature patterns and details – scales, fur etc.
6	**Pinch pot beasts 2** • Can create patterns using paint on a 3D surface. • Can apply decorative paint to a small sculpture to create detail.	• To manipulate malleable materials to make 3D sculpture and objects • To blend and join surfaces of malleable materials • To apply a range of patterns, textures and decorative finishes to malleable materials	Decorate both pinch-pots using poster paints, metallic paints. Focus on painting basic colours and then adding detail to the features and patterns created in previous sessions. • Use a range of colours. • Select appropriate sized paintbrush.

Year 3 Background knowledge

Down our street

Viewfinders are easily created by folding an A4 sheet of black card in half and carefully cutting a small rectangle at the centre of the crease. When opened out, the larger rectangle at the centre is used as the viewfinder.

For collage work it is always useful to have a collection of magazines and newspapers from which images can be cut. Accurate cutting out of images is a key skill for children to develop in art and design. Pictures can be stored either by colour or by theme for use in art and design projects.

Butterflies

Introduce a digital element to the topic: paint software has the function to create symmetrical patterns and this can be used to create digital butterflies for printing. In addition, most software also has a function that allows creations of stamps. A drawn butterfly design on the computer can easily be turned into a stamp and used to create multiple images and prints.

If possible look at the butterfly images of Rebecca Coles (www.rebeccajcoles.co.uk).

Van Gogh

Vincent Van Gogh was a Dutch painter who lived in the latter half of the nineteenth century. Although Van Gogh painted hundreds of pictures during his life (some of his masterpieces were created in one day), it is believed that he only sold one painting during his lifetime.

Recommended websites:
www.vangoghgallery.com
www.nationalgallery.org.uk/artists/vincent-van-gogh
www.vggallery.com

Mighty beasts

Animal bodies are made up of many shapes. Children learn not to draw a finished outline straight away, but instead to sketch rough shapes based on a simple skeleton and then adding ovals to create the body shape. Children should be encouraged to study a range of photographs of animals when drawing them.

Celtic crafts

There are many images of Celtic crafts available to view via search engines, or by looking at the collections of: The British Museum, The National Gallery of Wales, National Galleries Scotland and the Victoria and Albert Museum (either in person or online). Images of the work of George Bain, sometimes called the father of modern Celtic design can also be found on the internet.

Weaving vocabulary

Weaving	The process of forming cloth or fabric on a loom by interlacing yarn or thread (or, as in this case, paper).
Loom	A frame for weaving yarn or thread into cloth or fabric.
Warp	Threads running lengthwise on the loom. The warp is placed on the loom prior to beginning the weaving process.
Weft	Threads that are weaved across the warp threads to form the web.
Web	The cloth or fabric produced by weaving.

Further information about weaving is available in the Year 5 units of work.

Where the Wild Things Are by Maurice Sendak

The story focuses on a young boy named Max, who, after dressing in his wolf costume, wreaks havoc through his household and is disciplined by being sent to his bedroom. Max's bedroom undergoes a mysterious transformation into a jungle environment, and he winds up sailing to an island inhabited by malicious beasts known as the 'Wild Things'. After successfully intimidating the creatures, Max is hailed as the King of the Wild Things and enjoys a playful romp with his subjects; however, he decides to return home, to the Wild Things' dismay. After arriving in his bedroom, Max discovers a hot supper waiting for him.

Year 4 Long-term planning

Aim 1: Exploring and creating

The National Curriculum states that children should be taught...with creativity, experimentation and an increasing awareness of different kinds of art, craft and design:
- to create sketch books to record their observations.

Select and record from first-hand observation and experience.

Use their imagination and originality to explore ideas for different purposes.

Record, annotate and modify work in their sketchbooks by:
- recording from observation, memory and their imagination
- trying out and evaluating their ideas
- designing for a range of different ideas and products.

Children experience and learn about:
- landscape painting
- abstract art
- heraldry and Coats of Arms
- embroidery and tapestry
- making masks
- creating a diorama.

Aim 2: Skills and techniques

The National Curriculum states that children should be taught:
- to develop their techniques, including their control and their use of materials.
- to improve their mastery of art and design techniques, including drawing, painting and sculpture with a range of materials.

To improve their mastery of techniques such as drawing, painting, sculpture and collage with materials such as pencil, charcoal, paint, clay, textiles and ICT. Children develop their artistic techniques in:
- drawing from observation, memory and their imagination
- drawing lines and shape with increasing accuracy and detail
- cutting and arranging paper to make compositions
- using watercolour paint to create landscapes
- beginning to show and awareness of depth and perspective in their paintings
- printing using stencils
- creating collage by combining a range of different materials and media
- making masks from a range of materials
- sewing and stitching to create embroidery and tapestry
- using a range of arts and craft materials to apply finishes to their work.

Aim 3: Evaluate and analyse

The National Curriculum states that children should be taught:
- to create sketch books to record their observations and use them to review and revisit ideas.

Reflect on their own and others' work, comparing ideas and methods and adapting their work accordingly.

Describe how their work might develop further.

Throughout the units of work children should be encouraged to record, annotate and modify their work at all stages of the creative process creating a personal source of information and ideas, including:
- trying out different ideas and designs in their sketchbooks and identifying ways in which their work can be improved upon
- deciding on the best design *from their sketchbook* and using this to inform future work
- using their sketchbook to record *their own work and to include* ideas and work of other artists (this can include photographs, pictures of other works of art, examples of different media and techniques)
- using their sketchbooks to experiment with using different media and practising different skills and techniques.

Aim 4: Art and artists

The National Curriculum states that children should be taught:
- about the greatest artists, architects and designers in history.

Explore the work of artists, craft makers, and designers working in different times and cultures, including examples selected for them to view and through visits to museums and galleries and on-line collections.

Children learn about the works of a range of artists, including:
- Piet Mondrian
- Joan Miro
- Gustav Klimt,
- Henri Matisse
- Paul Klee
- Leonid Afremov
- Claude Monet
- David Hockney
- L.S. Lowry
- Georges Seurat
- Henri Rousseau.

Overview of progression in Year 4

Throughout the units in Year 4, children are:

- Using sketchbooks to collect and record visual information and ideas from different sources.
- Working from a variety of sources including observation, photographs and digital images.

Drawing

Through drawing a range of doodles, children are:

- Making marks and lines with a wide range of drawing implements including: graphite pencils (5B–5H), charcoal, colouring pencils, wax crayons, pastels (chalk & oil) and pens.
- Using different grades of pencil and other implements to create lines, draw different shapes and forms and to produce variations in tone.
- Exploring ways in which surface detail can be added to drawings through applying different patterns and textures, including shading and hatching.

Painting

Through drawing a range of doodles, children are:

- Creating imaginative work from a variety of sources e.g. observational drawing, themes, inspirational works of art.

Through their study of landscape paintings, children are:

- Creating imaginative work from a variety of sources e.g. observational drawing, themes, inspirational works of art.
- Developing a painting from a drawing, including sketchbook ideas.
- Creating different effects and textures using a range of techniques and paints, including blocking in colour and creating washes.
- Developing an awareness of composition, scale and proportion in their paintings.
- Using simple perspective in their work using a single focal point and horizon.

Through creating a number of rainforest paintings, children are:

- Creating imaginative work from a variety of sources e.g. observational drawing, themes, inspirational works of art.
- Developing a painting from a drawing, including sketchbook ideas.
- Creating different effects and textures using a range of techniques and paints.
- Extending knowledge of colour theory to complementary and contrasting colours.
- Developing an awareness of composition, scale and proportion in their paintings.

Printing

Through learning about the later works of Henri Matisse, children are:

- Using initial sketchbook ideas to create motifs that are made into printing blocks and stencils.
- Creating different printing effects by using: repeating patterns, rotation and colour overlays.

Year 4 Complete 'Overview of progression' is provided on the CD-ROM, including 'Collage and textiles' and 'Sculpture' objectives.

Medium-term planning: 1. Doodles

This unit of work encourages children to draw as much as possible. Doodling is a great, fun way for children to express themselves and also to develop greater skills in using drawing media.

YEAR 4

W	Outcomes	Objectives	Skills and understanding
1	**Scribble pictures** • Can create a continuous line scribble drawing to which blocks of colour are added.	• To develop greater control and confidence in using a range of drawing tools and media • To use painting techniques for different purposes	Create a continuous line scribble picture without the pencil leaving the paper. Add colours using these rules: • Only use three colours • No adjacent shape should have the same colour. This requires problem solving and planning ahead.
2	**Doodles Part 1** • Can create a detailed drawing consisting of many doodles of geometric shapes. • Can add colour using wax crayons or oil pastels.	• To develop greater control and confidence in using a range of drawing tools and media • To respond to imagination through drawing • To understand the qualities and effects of a range of drawing media	Begin anywhere on the paper, using fine-line pens, and start drawing doodles which are geometric shapes (circles, squares, triangles etc.). Once the paper is full of doodles, add colour using wax crayons.
3	**Doodles Part 2** • Can create a monochrome doodle of organic shapes. • Can fill the doodle shapes using a range of patterns and textures.	(As session 2)	Building on the previous session, create more doodles. However these doodles must be organic shapes (squiggly, natural shapes, no straight lines). Once complete, fill in the doodles using a range of patterns and textures (dots, dashes, lines, cross-hatching, diagonals) to create a monochrome doodle.
4	**Abstract Mondrian** • Can create an abstract composition of geometric shapes in the style of Piet Mondrian.	• To develop greater control and confidence in using a range of drawing tools and media • To respond to what is observed or remembered through drawing • To understand the qualities and effects of a range of drawing media • To understand the effect of combining different media	Create a square template to draw around with a thick black felt-tipped pen. The template is always placed so that its sides are parallel to the sides of the paper being used, resulting in all lines being either vertical or horizontal. Multiple shapes are drawn using the template to create many rectangles and squares. Squares and rectangles are then coloured blue, red or yellow using oil pastels. All other shapes are left white.
5	**Joan Miro: Abstract** • Can create an abstract drawing of either an animal or person in the style of Joan Miro.	(As session 4) • To explore the work of great artists in history	Show a range of abstract works by the Spanish artist Joan Miro. Create an abstract doodle based on an animal or a person using either oil pastels or wax crayons, using large loops and circles to create the figure. Colour most of the drawing, again using pastels or crayons then add a colour wash to the whole composition.
6	**Gustav Klimt: *Portrait of Adele Bloch*** • Can combine a colour portrait photograph with a background of patterns and doodles to create an image in the style of Gustav Klimt.	(As session 5) • To reproduce the work of an artist using collage materials	**Sketchbooks**: Experience drawing different shapes, spirals and patterns using a range of different drawing tools. Combine a cut-out self-portrait photograph with a background of swirls and patterns using gold, silver, yellow, orange and black drawing pens in the style of Gustav Klimt.

Notes:
Digital art: These sessions can be successfully delivered using a paint software package to carry out all the tasks digitally.

Medium-term planning: 2. Landscapes

YEAR 4

In this unit of work children develop their skills and technique when using watercolour paints. This is achieved through a study of landscape paintings of famous artists.

W	Outcomes	Objectives	Skills and understanding
1	***The Flora on the Heath*: Paul Klee** • Can apply various techniques of applying watercolour paint to create an abstract landscape.	• To respond to what is observed or remembered through painting • To understand the qualities and effects of a range of painting media • To use painting techniques for different purposes • To learn about the work of artists from different times and cultures	Children examine the image by Paul Klee. Focus on how the sky has been created using 'wet on wet' technique. Demonstrate how to use watercolour tablets and how to 'load' the brush with paint. Use wet on wet technique to create a 'wash' for the sky. Use 'wet on dry' to create small squares to represent the different plants on the heath. Use 'dry on dry' technique to add further detail to the painting.
2	***Sunset* paintings: Leonid Afremov** • Can apply various techniques of applying watercolour paint to create a sunset painting.	(As session 1) • To respond to imagination through painting	Show examples of paintings of sunset patterns as a stimulus. Use wet on wet technique to create the sky and the land. The horizon line is where the sky meets the land. Using black watercolour paint and either wet on dry or dry brush technique, add painted silhouettes on to the area around the horizon line.
3	***Water Lilies*: Claude Monet** • Can create their own version of *Water Lilies* by Monet using watercolour paints. • Show a developing understanding of perspective when painting landscapes.	(As session 2)	Learn about impressionist painting through studying *Water Lilies*, 1905. Mix a range of blues, purples and greens using watercolours then apply as a wash to give the impression of water. Use a finer brush and 'wet on dry' paint in reeds and water lilies creating impressions rather than exact shapes.
4	**Aerial perspective: *Garrowby Hill*: David Hockney** • Can sketch a country landscape using wax resistant crayons. • Can add blocks of colour using varying saturated watercolours.	• To understand the effect of combining different media • To use painting techniques for different purposes • To learn about the work of artists from different times and cultures	Learn about how colour is used in aerial perspective and that colours are stronger nearer to the foreground. Wax crayons are used to provide outlines and detail based on observations of the *Garrowby Hill* painting.
5	**Urban landscape: *Industrial Landscape*: Lowry** • Can create an industrial landscape in the style of L.S. Lowry. • Can use perspective in their painting.	• To respond to imagination through painting • To use sketching to plan a composition • To learn about the work of artists from different times and cultures	Understand that landscape paintings are not confined to countryside and look at the urban landscape paintings of L.S. Lowry. When using perspective in painting: Buildings become smaller with less detail and colours fade as they get further away from the foreground. Create an industrial landscape from imagination.
6	***Sunday Afternoon on the Island of La Grand Jatte*: Georges Seurat** • Can create a landscape painting in the style of Seurat to demonstrate learning about watercolour and perspective over the previous sessions.	(As session 2)	Identify the foreground, middle ground and background and apply to own work. Consolidate their knowledge about how to create perspective, reflected in size of figures, use of colour and detail. Learn about the technique of 'pointillism' which allows the eye to mix the colour.

Notes:
Digital art: Using one of the new more sophisticated paint packages it is possible to deliver these sessions digitally using a computer.

Medium-term planning: 3. Matisse – Painting with scissors

This unit of work focuses around the later works of Henri Matisse when he was 'painting with scissors'. This is an opportunity to extend and consolidate children's skills and techniques in paper collage and printing using stencils.

W	Outcomes	Objectives	Skills and understanding
1	**Goldfish bowl** • Can create a paper collage based on a painting by Henri Matisse.	• To combine a range of materials to create a collage • To represent natural or man-made objects using collage materials • To explore the work of great artists in history • To reproduce the work of an artist using collage materials	Understand about the life and work of Henri Matisse and why towards the end of his life he 'painted with scissors'. Understand that collage is an art form that involves creating an image through assembling a range of materials, paper and found objects that are glued to paper. Create a collage background assembling a range of different papers of different colour and texture.
2	**Dancing snails** • Can create a paper collage based on a painting by Henri Matisse. • Can create a collage background by overlapping paper. • Can create a focus for the composition by cutting out a human figure.	• To use sketching to plan a composition • To create a design for a specific purpose • To represent natural or man-made objects using collage materials • To reproduce the work of an artist using collage materials	Learn about another two famous works of art by Henri Matisse: *The Snail* and *Icarus*. Create a background by assembling and layering different types of papers to create a snail collage. Draw the constituent parts of a human figure. They experiment with placing and moving the figure to create an expression of dance.
3	**Positive and negative space collage** • Can create a symmetrical paper cut-out design.	• To combine a range of materials to create a collage	Draw a pattern on A5 paper that is cut out and then placed on one half of A4 paper. Cut-outs are removed from paper and placed on opposite sides of A4 paper to create a symmetrical design in contrasting colours.
4	**Stencils: Using a pounce** • Can make and use a pounce when printing. • Can experiment with using a pounce and stencils to create a range of images.	• To know that the printing process can result in repeated images • To know that printing can be applied to many different surfaces	Make a pounce by using old rags to stuff a sock to make the pounce. Gain experience of using a pounce to apply ink to a ready-made stencil so that clear images are created.
5	**Stencils: Matisse dancer** • Can create a stencil of a dancer from drawing. • Can print multiple images using a stencil and a pounce.	• To know that the printing process can result in repeated images • To know that printing can be applied to many different surfaces	Draw the constituent parts of a human figure. Experiment with placing and moving the figure to create an expression of dance. This is then drawn around and cut out using a craft knife to create a stencil.
6	**Final composition: Dancers** • Can apply their knowledge of collage and stencil printing to create a composition that depicts a number of dancers.	• To combine a range of materials to create a collage • To reproduce the work of an artist using collage materials	Use both stencilled images from the previous session and paper 'cut-out' images of dancers to create the composition. Can work collaboratively to produce large scale compositions combining the work of several people.

YEAR 4

Medium-term planning: 4. Masquerade

This unit of work focuses on making masks. It allows children to design two different masks – one for a party and one designed around a curriculum topic.

W	Outcomes	Objectives	Skills and understanding
1	**Fancy dress mask** • Can create a design for a fancy dress mask based on a theme decided by the whole class.	• To respond to imagination through drawing • To use sketching to plan a composition • To design and make for a particular purpose	A theme is decided for the party. List what are the key features of a good party mask. Sketchbooks: The opportunity to try out a number of different ideas before settling on a chosen design.
2	**Fancy dress mask: Photograph masks** • Can make a fancy dress mask based on an original design.	• To create 3D objects from 2D materials • To use a range of adhesive and joining techniques when creating sculpture • To understand the importance of using tools appropriately and safely	Transfer the mask design from the sketchbook on to a photograph. Copy it on to card. Cut out holes for the eyes and mouth. Using sketchbook design as a guide, apply a base coating of paint to their mask.
3	**Fancy dress mask: Adding detail** • Can use a selection of art materials to add detail and embellishment to a mask.	• To create 3D objects from 2D materials • To create a range of decorative finishes	Add detail to the mask whilst still following the original design. Use a range of finishing and embellishing products such as crepe or tissue paper, glitter, sequins, metallic paints, to enhance their mask.
4	**Designing the mask** • Can design a mask based on a topic currently being studying.	• To respond to imagination through drawing • To use sketching to plan a composition • To design and make for a particular purpose	Provide the opportunity to handle masks or photographs of, different masks from around the world. Discuss and identify what elements make a good mask. Using photographs related to the topic, design a mask using a face template.
5	**Making the mask** • Can using a range of joining techniques to add structure to a 3D mask. • Can strengthen a mask by adding layers of papier-mâché.	• To create 3D objects from 2D materials • To use a range of adhesive and joining techniques when creating sculpture • To understand the importance of using tools appropriately and safely	Using their design from the previous session, children create the structure of their mask from a ready-made face mask. They use card to add additional features such as ears, horns and hats. The mask and additional features are strengthened by adding layers of papier-mâché.
6	**Finishing the mask** • Can use a selection of art materials to add detail and embellishment to a mask.	• To create 3D objects from 2D materials • To create a range of decorative finishes	Add detail, as desired, to the mask whilst still following the original design. Use a range of finishing and embellishing products such as crepe or tissue paper, glitter, sequins, metallic paints, to enhance their mask.

Notes:

Sessions 1–3: The theme for the party could come from a book or topic currently being studied.

Sessions 4–6: This can be adapted to suit a range of topics – Diwali masks from the Ramayana, Egyptian Gods and Goddesses, animal masks.

Ready-made face masks can be purchased from most educational suppliers. A mask template is also available on the CD-ROM and on the web site (www.scholastic.co.uk/100artanddesign).

Medium-term planning: 5. Heraldry

In this unit, children learn about Coats of Arms and their meaning and symbolism. They develop their skills in textiles and sewing by creating a tapestry based on their own design for a Coat of Arms.

YEAR 4

W	Outcomes	Objectives	Skills and understanding
1	**Coat of Arms: The shield** • Can design a Coat of Arms for a shield. • Can create a base design for a shield using large card and paint.	• To respond to imagination through drawing • To respond to imagination through painting • To use sketching to plan a composition • To learn about the work of artists from different times and cultures	Learn about how 'Coats of Arms' came about in the Middle Ages. Show a range of different shield designs and learn about the meanings of different colours used on shields. Plan shield design in their sketchbooks using colours that represent themselves.
2	**Coat of Arms: The symbols** • Can design symbols for a personal Coat of Arms. • Can draw large scale symbols using thick marker pens.	• To develop greater control and confidence in using a range of drawing tools and media • To respond to what is observed or remembered through drawing • To create a design for a specific purpose	Learn about symbolism on a Coat of Arms. Provided with a range of ready-made symbols and the opportunity to design symbols of their own in their sketchbooks, they complete their design for their personal Coat of Arms.
3	**Coat of Arms: Putting it together** • Can combine cut-out drawings with a painted shield to create a Coat of Arms.	• To combine a range of materials to create a collage • To understand the qualities and effects of a range of painting media • To understand the effect of combining different media	Complete Coat of Arms by using a sketchbook design when creating their shield. Cutting out and colouring the symbols for their shield to achieve a high quality finish. Combining symbols with shield from session 1 to create their own Coat of Arms. The finished shields are laminated and displayed in the classroom.
4	**Tapestry: Binca stitching** • Can create a range of different cross-stitches. • Can create a patterned border on a large embroidery sheet.	• To decorate fabrics in a number of different ways and finishes • To apply a range of sewing techniques and stitches to combine and decorate fabrics	Show and practise a range of embroidery cross-stitches for use on a tapestry. They create a decorative border on their Binca sheet using a range of stitches and coloured threads.
5	**Tapestry – felt coat of arms** • Can create a personal Coat of Arms in felt. • Can sew a felt Coat of Arms to the centre of an embroidery sheet.	• To draw and cut out a fabric pattern • To decorate fabrics in a number of different ways and finishes • To apply a range of sewing techniques and stitches to combine and decorate fabrics	Use designs from previous sessions to draw fabric pattern to use when cutting out felt shapes for their Coat of Arms. Learn how to attach the pattern to the felt fabric using pins and then cut around the pattern. Elements are glued to the shield shape; this is then sewn on to the Binca using a small running stitch.
6	**Additional components** • Can add additional felt pieces to an embroidery sheet to elaborate and decorate their tapestry.	• To decorate fabrics in a number of different ways and finishes • To apply a range of sewing techniques and stitches to combine and decorate fabrics	Further develop and consolidate their skills learnt in session 5 by creating additional elements for their tapestry. Each additional piece of felt can be decorated and detail added using a range of decorative stitches.

Notes:
There are obvious cross-curricular links in this unit with history, e.g. Middle Ages, knights and castles. A template to help children design their own Coat of Arms can be found at www.scholastic.co.uk/100artanddesign.

Medium-term planning: 6. Rainforests

This unit of work is based around the theme of rainforests. Children learn how to make a traditional mola and to create a rainforest diorama based on a Henri Rousseau painting.

W	Outcomes	Objectives	Skills and understanding
1	**Complementary coloured chameleons** • Can draw intricate designs and add colour to shown an understanding of complementary colours to a stencil outline.	• To respond to imagination through drawing • To mix and match a range of primary and secondary colours	Draw a chameleon outline onto card, use bold lines and make the shape large enough to cut out. Use the cut shape as a stencil and fill an A3 piece of paper with shapes. Colour and pattern each shapes using complementary colours, to display an understanding of colours on the colour wheel.
2	**Rainforest mola 1** • Can draw an outline design of an animal of the rainforest. • Can use a design to create a fabric pattern.	• To respond to what is observed or remembered through drawing • To respond to imagination through drawing • To create a design for a specific purpose • To draw and cut out a fabric pattern	Sketchbooks: Children sketch out several designs for an animal of the rainforest before settling on a final outline design. Drawing an outline of the chosen animal on to thin paper to create a fabric pattern.
3	**Rainforest mola 2** • Can cut out fabric from a pattern they have designed.	• To draw and cut out a fabric pattern • To apply a range of sewing techniques and stitches to combine and decorate fabrics	Cut out the shape from fabric, using pattern, with sharp fabric scissors. Use the technique of 'tacking' to temporarily attach the two pieces of materials to each other. Permanently secure the two pieces using small running stitch. Select an appropriate thread to create an artistic effect.
4	**Rainforest mola (Part 3)** • Can use stitching to combine two or more fabric designs to each other.	• To decorate fabrics in a number of different ways and finishes • To apply a range of sewing techniques and stitches to combine and decorate fabrics	Continue to practise using a small neat running stitch to secure layers of felt to create the mola. Experiment with different types of stitches for decorative effects. Add embellishments such as beads, sequins and ribbons. Cut the fabric edges into a fringe for effect.
5	**Rousseau diorama 1** • Can sketch and paint a jungle scene in which there is a clear background, middle ground and foreground. • Can use colour and aerial perspective to give a feeling of depth in a painting.	• To respond to imagination through painting • To use sketching to plan a composition • To use painting techniques for different purposes • To learn about the work of artists from different times and cultures	Introduce the jungles paintings of Henri Rousseau. Understand that such a composition consists of a foreground, middle ground and background and that artists use colour as a form of aerial perspective to give the impression of depth. Sketch and paint their own jungle scene focusing on creating a background, middle ground and foreground using watercolours.
6	**Rousseau diorama 2** • Can use an original painting as a stimulus to create a diorama. • Can create three separate paintings that are combined to form a diorama.	• To mix and match a range of primary and secondary colours • To learn about the work of artists from different times and cultures	Using the painting from session 5 as a stimulus, create three separate paintings on card to enable the creation of a diorama.

Notes:
Rainforest molas: the best fabric to use for these sessions is felt. Use complete squares for the background of the mola (normally black).
For the diorama, the three pieces of card can be glued to lengths of 10mm × 10mm wood to create depth.

Year 4 Background knowledge

Landscapes

Landscape painting is the depiction of natural landscapes such as hills, valley, mountains, islands and coasts.

Wet on wet technique is used to create a wash. A wash is a very thin coat of paint. You can still see the paper underneath a wash as it is transparent. Washes are good for flat, light areas like sky or a large body of water.

Wet on dry technique is used for painting areas that require greater control and use of saturated colours, for example in the foreground of a painting.

Dry brush technique involves blotting the brush dry and is used to create interesting textures and fine lines, and can be used for very detailed work.

Matisse

Henri Matisse was a famous French artist who primarily worked during the first part of the twentieth century. He started off as a traditional landscape and still-life painter. As his style developed he became influenced by the works of impressionists and soon began to use bold and bright colours in his work (Fauvism). As he grew much older he was confined to his bed and used paper cut-outs as a means of creating works of art.

Key works:
- *Icarus* (1947)
- *The Fall of Icarus* (1943)
- *The Snail* (1953)
- *The Goldfish* (1912)

Heraldry

Coat of Arms

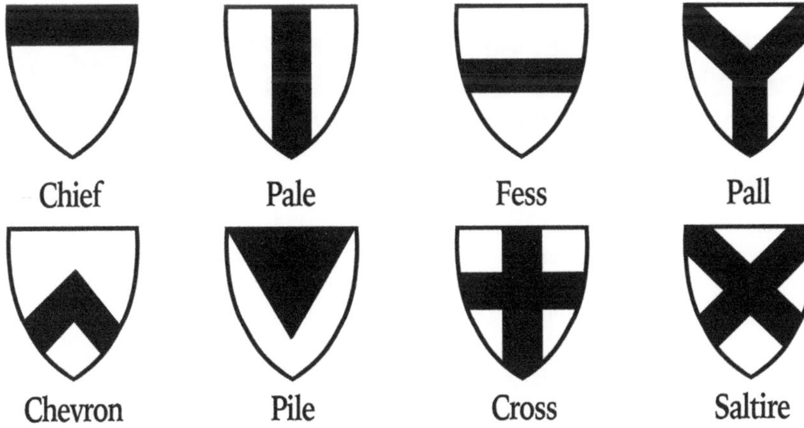

These are some of the basic shield designs for Coats of Arms.

Colours that are used on coats of arms and what they are thought to signify:

Yellow or Gold – Generosity
White or Silver – Peace
Black – Grief
Blue – Loyalty & Truthfulness
Red – Military Might
Green – Hope, Joy & Loyalty
Purple – Royalty

Heraldic animals and symbols and their meanings

Bear – Protective
Bee – Hard working
Cross – Christian
Crown – Royal
Dog – Loyal
Dragon – Defender of Treasure
Eagle – Leader
Fox – Clever
Griffin (part eagle, part lion) – Brave
Hand – Fair
Heart – Sincerity
Lightning – Decisiveness
Lion – Courageous
Moon – Calm and peaceful
Pelican – Generous
Stag – Peace loving
Star – Important
Sun – Glory
Sword – Warlike
Tiger – Fierce
Tower or Castle – Protective
Unicorn – Extremely Courageous

Rainforests

Molas are the most famous native artwork from Panama in Central America. Originally a mola formed the front and back part of a women's blouse. Originally the patterns of molas were geometrical designs; however, over the past fifty years other designs using animals and flowers have been used. Most molas feature red, orange and black as their predominant colours. Molas are created through successive layering of sheets of fabrics which are stitched together – a process called appliqué. Additional stitches are added to the base layer of fabric (normally black) to decorate and embellish the spaces.

Year 5 Long-term planning

Aim 1: Exploring and creating

The National Curriculum states that children should be taught… with creativity, experimentation and an increasing awareness of different kinds of art, craft and design:
- to create sketchbooks to record their observations.

Select and record from first hand observation and experience.

Use their imagination and originality to explore ideas for different purposes.

Record, annotate and modify work in their sketchbooks by:
- recording from observation, memory and their imagination
- trying out and evaluating their ideas
- designing for a range of different ideas and products.

Children experience and learn about:
- the artist and designer William Morris
- the art of painting flowers
- weaving
- the art of Wassily Kandinsky
- art from different sculptures
- designing and drawing maps.

Aim 2: Skills and techniques

The National Curriculum states that children should be taught:
- to develop their techniques, including their control and their use of materials.
- to improve their mastery of art and design techniques, including drawing, painting and sculpture with a range of materials.

To improve their mastery of techniques such as drawing, painting. sculpture and collage with materials such as pencil, charcoal, paint, clay, textiles and ICT. Children develop their artistic techniques in:
- drawing from observation, memory and their imagination
- drawing lines and shape with increasing accuracy and detail
- designing for a range of purposes
- mixing and applying different paint colours
- drawing maps
- illuminated letter designing
- block printing
- creating sculpture from a range of materials
- creating a clay bas relief
- different types of weaving.

Aim 3: Evaluate and analyse

The National Curriculum states that children should be taught:
- to create sketchbooks to record their observations and use them to review and revisit ideas.

Reflect on their own and others' work, comparing ideas and methods and adapting their work accordingly.

Describe how their work might develop further.

Throughout the units of work children should be encouraged to record, annotate and modify their work at all stages of the creative process creating a personal source of information and ideas, including:
- trying out different ideas and designs in their sketchbooks and identifying ways in which their work can be improved upon
- deciding on the best design *from their* sketchbook and using this to inform future work
- using their sketchbook to record *their own work and to include* ideas and work of other artists (this can include photographs, pictures of other works of art, examples of different media and techniques)
- using their sketchbooks to experiment with using different media and practising different skills and techniques.

Aim 4: Art and artists

The National Curriculum states that children should be taught:
- about the greatest artists, architects and designers in history.

Explore the work of artists, craft makers, and designers working in different times and cultures, including examples selected for them to view and through visits to museums and galleries and on-line collections.

Children learn about the works of a range of artists, including:
- William Morris
- Tom Yelland
- Vincent Van Gogh
- Wassily Kandinsky.

Overview of progression in Year 5

Drawing

Throughout the units in Year 5, children are:

- Using sketchbooks to collect and record visual information and ideas from different sources.
- Working from a variety of sources including observation, photographs and digital images.

Through studying art from a range of different cultures, children are:

- Making marks and lines with a wide range of drawing implements including colouring pencils, wax crayons, pastels (chalk & oil) and pens.
- Exploring ways in which surface detail can be added to drawings through applying different patterns and textures, including shading and hatching.

Through drawing maps and making 3D models of maps, children are:

- Making marks and lines with a wide range of drawing implements including graphite pencil and fine-line pens.
- Explore ways in which surface detail can be added to drawings through applying different patterns and textures, including shading and hatching.

Painting

Through creating a series of flower paintings in 'Blossoming out', children are:

- Creating imaginative work from a variety of sources such as observational drawings and inspirational works of art.
- Developing a painting from a drawing, including sketchbook ideas.
- Extending their knowledge of colour theory through mixing primary and secondary colours, tints, tones and shades.
- Developing an awareness of composition, scale and proportion in their paintings.

Through making 3D representations of Kandinsky-inspired paintings, children are:

- Creating imaginative work from a variety of sources including inspirational works of art.
- Creating different effects and textures using a range of techniques and paints.

Through studying art from a range of different cultures, children are:

- Creating imaginative work from a variety of sources e.g. observational drawing, themes, inspirational works of art.
- Developing a painting from a drawing, including sketchbook ideas.
- Creating different effects and textures using a range of techniques and paints.
- Extending knowledge of colour theory to include tints, tones and shades.

Printing

Through making their hand-printed William Morris inspired wallpaper, children are:

- Creating printing blocks based on motifs that they have designed and modified.
- Creating prints using a relief method.
- Creating printing patterns that are repeated or feature overlays.

Year 5 Complete 'Overview of progression' is provided on the CD-ROM, including 'Collage and textiles' and 'Sculpture' objectives.

YEAR 5

Medium-term planning: 1. William Morris

This unit of work is based on the work and designs of the Victorian designer and artist William Morris. Children study his illuminated letter designs and create a clay bas relief illuminated letter. The remainder of the unit of work offers a series of printing workshops in which children are introduced to block printing.

W	Outcomes	Objectives	Skills and understanding
1	**Illuminated letters** • Can create a design for an illuminated letter based on the designs of William Morris.	• To respond to what is observed or remembered through drawing • To create a design for a specific purpose	Sketchbooks: Use to sketch and evaluate different designs using a range of stimuli. Suggest ways to improve designs before finalising their illuminated letter design.
2	**Illuminated relief sculpture** • Can create a clay bas relief sculpture based on sketchbook designs.	• To design and make for a particular purpose following a sketchbook design • To understand the importance of using tools appropriately and safely • To manipulate malleable materials to make 2D compositions • To blend and join surfaces of malleable materials	Create a square clay tile by evenly rolling a slab of clay between two guide sticks. Then accurately cut a square tile of clay. Explore different ways to add decorative features to a tile to form a clay bas relief. Develop techniques for joining pieces of clay together by roughing surfaces and the use of slip.
3	**Motifs** • Can represent individual motifs from the printed wallpaper designs of William Morris.	• To know that making a print involves transferring an image from one surface to another • To know that the printing process can result in repeated images	Use a viewfinder to locate and isolate a single motif for closer study. Use sketchbooks to make close observations and detailed drawings. Use fine brush skills to add watercolour paint to a drawn motif design using a small brush and 'wet on dry' technique.
4	**Designing a motif** • Can create a design for a block print.	• To respond to what is observed or remembered through drawing • To create a design for a specific purpose	Use sketchbooks to understand what a motif is and creating a simple motif design that can easily be turned into a block print design.
5	**Creating the print block** • Can create a printing block based on sketchbook designs.	• To design and make for a particular purpose following a sketchbook design	Copy a motif design on to a neoprene square. Accurately cut out motif design using scissors and/or a craft knife. Reassemble cut-out motif accurately on to thick card square to create identical motif design. Test a block print for the quality of print.
6	**Wallpaper printing** • Work collaboratively to use printing blocks to create large sheets of wallpaper.	• To know that making a print involves transferring an image from one surface to another • To know that the printing process can result in repeated images • To understand an apply a range of printmaking processes – block printing	Using roller and ink to 'ink up' their printing block. Investigate different ways of producing patterns using a block print. For this collaborative composition, children should plan their method of working carefully. For example, specific roles within the group and the type of pattern that is to be created.

Notes:
Session 2: Clay tile cutters can be purchased from educational suppliers.
Session 5: It is recommended that self-adhesive neoprene is used, this is sometimes advertised as 'fun foam'.
Session 6: This provides cross-curricular opportunities with mathematics – rotation and translation of shapes.
Sessions 4–6: These sessions can be carried out using paint software; a design is created and turned into a 'stamp' which is then used to create repeating patterns.

Medium-term planning: 2. Blossoming out

This unit of work gives children the opportunity to further their knowledge and application of colour-mixing theory. They learn how to mix shades and tints of colours through a series of activities based around flower paintings.

YEAR 5

W	Outcomes	Objectives	Skills and understanding
1	**Observational drawing** • Can use their sketchbooks to draw from observation. • Can add colour to drawings using watercolour paints.	• To develop greater control and confidence in using a range of drawing tools and media • To respond to what is observed or remembered through drawing	Sketchbooks: Make Close observation and detailed drawing of flowers, adding appropriate colour.
2	**Mixed media flowers** • Can create mixed flower designs from tissue paper and acrylic paint.	(As session 1) • To understand the effect of combining different media	Use ideas from sketchbook to inform the creative process. Use tissue paper to create petal shapes and add detail using acrylic paint.
3	**Finishing the flower 1** • Can complete a flower painting by continuing the shape, form and colour of the original.	• To respond to imagination through painting • To understand the qualities and effects of a range of painting media • To use painting techniques for different purposes • To mix and match a range of primary and secondary colours	Mix secondary colours to create the six basic colours on the colour wheel and match to everyday objects. Fine brush control and using different sized brushes to create detailed shapes and patterns.
4	**Finishing the flower 2** • Can complete a flower painting by continuing the shape, form and colour of the original. • Can mix a range of shades and tints of primary and secondary colours.	(As session 3)	Make a **shade** of a colour by adding successive amounts of black. Make a **tint** of a colour by adding successive amounts of white. Fine brush control and using different sized brushes to create detailed shapes and patterns.
5	**Sun and moon flowers** • Can sketch a large composition of sunflowers in the style of Van Gogh. • Can add colours creatively to show their understanding of warm and cool colours.	• To respond to what is observed or remembered through painting • To use sketching to plan a composition • To mix and match a range of primary and secondary colours • To learn about the work of artists from different times and cultures	Create a large sketch of sunflowers in a vase in the style of Van Gogh. Understand what is meant by warm and cool colours. Apply this knowledge when painting the picture. Once the sketch has been completed, it is vertically divided in half with one half being painted using cool colours, the other half using warm colours.
6	**In the style of Tom Yendell** • Using the work of Tom Yendell as an inspiration, children create a large scale fantasy flower composition.	(As session 5)	Use observations and knowledge of flower paintings to create a large scale composition. Combine large blocks of colour with fine detailed brushwork to create flower paintings. Extend knowledge of painting composition by creating focal points in the painting.

Notes:

Session 1: Provide the children with a range of flowers – tulips, lilies, freesias, and daffodils make good subjects.

Sessions 3–4: Children are provided with copies of flower paintings that have been ripped in half – they are challenged to complete the 'missing half' of the painting.

Session 6: There are several online videos of Tom Yendell overcoming his disability to create exceptional works of art with his mouth and feet. Featured work: *Silk Flowers* (www.tomyendell.co.uk).

Medium-term planning: 3. Weaving

YEAR 5

This unit of work offers a series of weaving workshops that will extend and consolidate children's knowledge about weaving and allow them to practise the skills and techniques involved in this craft.

W	Outcomes	Objectives	Skills and understanding
1	**Creating a loom** • Can make a simple cardboard weaving frame. • Can create the warp threads on a weaving loom.	• To make simple weaving looms and practice weaving skills	Create a cardboard loom using a piece of flat card, making equal-sized notches at each end, to run the warp through. Ensure that the string is tight when making the warp.
2	**Creating the weave** • Can create a weave by threading the weft through the warp. • Can create interesting weaving patterns and effects using a range of materials.	• To make simple weaving looms and practice weaving skills • To apply a range of sewing techniques and stitches to combine and decorate fabrics	Understand the correct weaving terminology: • Thread the weft through the warp by using the shuttle (tapestry needle) to create the cloth. • Use a fork to ensure that the individual strands of weft are close and tight together. • Use opportunities to add other appropriate materials to the weave and to change the colour and texture of the weft material.
3	**Twig weaving** • Can construct a loom from a 'Y' shaped twig. • Can weave using a 'twig loom' and a range of natural coloured threads.	• To make simple weaving looms and practice weaving skills • To apply a range of sewing techniques and stitches to combine and decorate fabrics	Apply the same principles, as above, to a natural object such as a twig. Create the warp Weave using the weft and shuttle.
4	**Mandala project 1** • Understand the role of Mandalas in Hinduism and Buddhism. • Can design their own mandala in their sketchbooks.	• To respond to what is observed or remembered through drawing • To create a design for a specific purpose	Use a compass for reference; draw a circle which is then divided into eight segments radiating from the centre. Create a number of designs for mandalas adding colour using pencils, recognising that designs need to be simple enough to be repeated in all eight segments.
5	**Mandala project 2** • Can use sketchbook designs to create Mandala design on a large paper plate. • Can add colour to the design using felt-tipped pens.	• To understand the effect of combining different media • To sketch to plan a composition	The final chosen design is transferred on to a circular paper plate and colour is added using felt-tipped pens.
6	**Mandala project 3** • Can create a circular loom using a large paper plate. • Can enhance the mandala design through weaving a range of brightly coloured materials.	• To make simple weaving looms and practice weaving skills • To apply a range of sewing techniques and stitches to combine and decorate fabrics	Create a circular weaving loom by: • Creating a hole in the centre of the plate and equally spaced notches around the edges – this allows the creation of the warp. • The weft is threaded through the warp as for other weaving activities using the shuttle.

Notes:

Session 1: Consolidates knowledge of weaving first taught in Year 3.

Session 2: Children should have access to strips of materials, ribbon offcuts and textiles that are flexible and can be used within the weave. As children progress with the weave, encourage them to change the colour and texture of the weft to create different patterns and effects.

Digital art: Using the symmetry tool in a paint package allows the creation of digital mandala.

Medium-term planning: 4. Kandinsky 3D

This unit of work uses the abstract work of Wassily Kandinsky as a stimulus for children to create a series of 3D sculptures.

W	Outcomes	Objectives	Skills and understanding
1	**Concentric circles, triangles and squares** • Understand and recognise abstract art as a genre. • Demonstrate and consolidate their knowledge of colour mixing techniques.	• To respond to imagination through painting • To use painting techniques for different purposes • To learn about the work of artists from different times and cultures	Display and discuss the work of Wassily Kandinsky. Using the works as a stimulus, children create their own concentric shapes painting on thick card. Discuss their use of colour, in particular their colour mixing throughout the session.
2	**3D Kandinsky** • Can transform a 2D image into a 3D sculpture using a range of cuts, bends and twists.	• To create 3D objects from 2D materials • To design and make for a particular purpose	Accurately cut concentric shapes into spirals so that they can become free-standing spiral structures. Investigate other ways of turning 2D art into 3D forms through cutting, bending, folding and joining different components of the painting.
3	**Abstract Kandinsky** • Can create an abstract art composition. • Consolidate their understanding of abstract art.	• To respond to imagination through painting • To use sketching to plan a composition • To use painting techniques for different purposes • To learn about the work of artists from different times and cultures	Use more examples of abstract work by Wassily Kandinsky as stimuli; children compose their own abstract painting made up of squares, rectangles, triangles and circles. Look for accurate drawing of geometric shapes while creating the abstract painting. Add blocks of colour to the shapes and finish shapes with decorative designs.
4 5	**Creating the sculpture** • Can create a 3D sculpture based on a 2D painting. • Can make a range of 3D shapes from sheet materials. • Can combine a range of 3D shapes and 2D shapes to make a sculpture.	• To create 3D objects from 2D materials • To design and make for a particular purpose • To create a range of decorative finishes	Use the abstract painting from the previous session as the stimulus for creating a 3D shape. Draw and create nets of shapes such as cubes, cuboids and rectangular prisms out of card. Form the nets into 3D shapes through cutting, scoring, folding and gluing. Cut out 2D shapes in thick card to create 3D representations of the painting. Add colour and pattern to 3D objects and shapes.
6	**Assembling the sculpture** • Can assemble their sculpture from the component shapes on to a thick card base.	• To use a range of adhesive and joining techniques when creating sculpture • To understand the importance of using tools appropriately and safely	Use a range of joining techniques such as gluing and making slots to assemble the sculpture. Assess and comment critically as to whether their sculpture is a true representation of their abstract painting.

Notes:

Session 1: If this unit is taught after 'Blossoming out' it provides an ideal opportunity for children to consolidate their knowledge of colour theory and colour mixing. Children could demonstrate their knowledge of primary and secondary colours, shades and tints and warm and cool colours. (Stimulus: *Colour Study – Squares and Concentric Circles*, 1913)

Sessions 4 & 5: Paper or polystyrene spheres and different-sized cardboard tubes are readily available from educational stockists and can act as 3D representations of circles. Children will need to be able to construct cubes, cuboids and prisms from card nets. Some components can be more 2D and can be cut out of card of differing thicknesses.

YEAR 5

Medium-term planning: 5. Art from other cultures

This unit of work gives children the opportunity to investigate pattern through a study of art from other cultures. The unit is also designed to reinforce the benefits of studying original art forms, trying out ideas and making notes in sketchbooks, before deciding on own final design.

W	Outcomes	Objectives	Skills and understanding
1	**Aboriginal 'Dreaming' paintings** • Can create an Aboriginal 'Dreaming' painting.	• To respond to imagination through painting • To use painting techniques for different purposes • To learn about the work of artists from different times and cultures	Identify common features: • X-ray of skeleton included • main colours used • methods of patterning (dots). Draw animal outline with skeleton and then add patterns using appropriate colours and cotton buds.
2	**Greek amphora** • Can create a design for a Greek vase using scratch paper. • Can create traditional Greek patterns and figures to decorate their vase.	• To respond to imagination through painting • To use painting techniques for different purposes • To learn about the work of artists and designers from different times and cultures	Study a range of photographs of Ancient Greek vases. Identify the different repeating patterns that are used and replicate them in sketchbooks. Invent own repeating patterns and sketch. Decide and draw a main figure or motif that will form the main part of the vase design.
3	**Arabic Mehndi patterns** • Can design their own intricate Mehndi hand pattern designs.	• To develop greater control and confidence in using a range of drawing tools and media • To create a design for a specific purpose • To learn about the work of artists and designers from different times and cultures	Study examples of Mehndi patterns and list key features of a good pattern. Trace around own hands on to cartridge paper and then add patterns using fine line pens. Assess designs against their agreed criteria for a good Mehndi design.
4	**Blue willow china plates** • Can create their 'willow pattern' design on a white paper plate using various shades and tints of blue.	• To respond to imagination through drawing • To use sketching to plan a composition • To create a design for a specific purpose	Consolidate principals of colour mixing and knowledge of how to mix shades and tints of blue. Listen to the poem *'Two Birds Flying High'* as a source of inspiration for their willow pattern design. Sketchbooks: Study pictures of willow designs and design the main elements of plate in sketchbooks before applying them to the paper plates.
5	**Native American totem pole** • Can use ideas from sketchbook to create a design for a totem pole. • Can combine thick markers, paint and pastels when adding colour to the design.	• To respond to imagination through drawing • To create a design for a specific purpose • To learn about the work of artists and designers from different times and cultures	Look at examples of this art form and discuss the meaning and symbolism. Sketchbooks: Study and draw different forms of nose and mouths that are found on totem poles before deciding on a final design for their totem pole. Several individual designs can be combined to make classroom displays
6	**Russian onion domes** • Can use ideas from sketchbook to design an 'onion domed tower'. • Can add colour, using washable ink (to provide strong colour) and glitter for finishing effect.	• To respond to what is observed or remembered through drawing • To respond to imagination through drawing • To create a design for a specific purpose • To learn about the work of artists and designers from different times and cultures	Sketchbooks: Draw different shapes of onion domes based on pictures and photographs provided. Focus on the different patterns and designs found on the buildings, in particular the designs for the windows. Sketches and ideas are used to inform final design.

Notes:
This unit of work presents ample opportunities for cross-curricular work in English, history and geography.
Session 4: This unit offers cross-curricular opportunities for storytelling and poetry linked to the blue willow pattern (see background notes).

Medium-term planning: 6. Mapping it out

Maps are one of the oldest forms of communication. This unit of work, based on maps of their local community, gives children the opportunity to further develop and consolidate both their drawing skills and their 3D construction techniques.

W	Outcomes	Objectives	Skills and understanding
1	**A map of me** • Can draw a map of their life so far combining words, pictures and symbols.	• To create a design for a specific purpose • To create maps, charts or diagrams to record observations or mental images	Sketchbooks: Children practise different drawing techniques for arrows and map lettering. They draw a depiction of themselves that they will use throughout the map.
2	**Fantasy map / Pirate map** • Can use their imagination to create a detailed fantasy map.	• To respond to imagination through drawing • To understand the effect of combining different media • To create maps, charts or diagrams to record observations or mental images	Provide photographs showing landscape features that could be included on the map. Use sketchbooks to design: • landscape and other features • buildings and places • mythical beasts or treasure troves. Ageing the mapping paper can be achieved by folding, creasing and painting with strong tea.
3	**Old style town map** • Can use their imagination to draw a map of what the map may have looked like 500 years ago.	• To respond to what is observed or remembered through drawing • To respond to imagination through drawing • To create maps, charts or diagrams to record observations or mental images	Examine and list the key features found on old town maps, look at current aerial photographs and maps of the local area. Analyse key features of maps (compass rose, date, and border). Sketchbooks: Practise designs for the key features of the map.
4	**Our local map** • Can apply collage techniques to combine a range of media to create a map of the local area.	• To respond to what is observed or remembered through drawing • To create maps, charts or diagrams to record observations or mental images • To combine a range of materials to create a collage	Sketch then paint landscape features of the local area (roads, rivers, fields etc.). Create designs for features e.g. trees that are photocopied and cut out for inclusion on the map. Add photographs / drawings of local landmarks to the map. Information panels, compass etc. can also be added to the final collage.
5 6	**3D modelling** • Can create a 3D 'model' of their local community.	• To create maps, charts or diagrams to record • To create 3D objects from 2D materials • To design and make for a particular purpose	Use a range of modelling materials and recycled materials to create small 3D models of buildings in the locality or fantasy buildings that they would like to be built (swimming pools etc.). Use knowledge of creating 3D shapes from nets to help in their creation of their model buildings. Use patterned and textured paper to create pathways, roads and other flat features on their square base.

Notes:
This unit can be taught in conjunction with units of study based on local history or geography.
An accurate 3D map of the local area depends upon creating an accurate base for the map. This is best achieved by greatly enlarging a map of the locality that has grid squares. Each enlarged square is then cut out, stuck on to thick card and given to an individual or group of children as their square that will be combines at the end to form the model. (This means that existing roads, rivers, parks etc. will join up on the finished model.) It is also a good idea to agree on colours or techniques to ensure that the roads, rivers, parks etc. match up in colour.
Session 1: Maps can take any form that the children want, e.g. the child can be at the centre with links to important areas of their life or the map can take the form of a journey from their birth day onwards. Teachers may need to be sensitive to the background of children in their class.
Sessions 3 onwards: These require access to maps and aerial photographs of the local area. Prior to these sessions, children should be given the opportunity to walk around the local area taking photographs of local landmarks and places of interest.

Year 5 Background knowledge

William Morris

William Morris is one of the most famous artist/designers of the Victorian Era. He was incredibly creative producing a range of decorative art including furniture, stained glass, textiles, tapestries wallpaper and lettering. William Morris once said: *'Have nothing in your house that you do not know to be useful, or believe to be beautiful.'*

Blossoming out

Primary colours: The three primary colours are red, yellow and blue; the only colours that cannot be made by mixing two other colours.

Secondary colours: The three secondary colours are green, orange and violet; they are each a mixture of two primary colours.

Warm colours: These are considered to be oranges, yellows, and reds.

Cool colours: These are considered to be blue, green and violet.

Complementary colours: Pairs of colours that are opposite each other on the colour wheel.

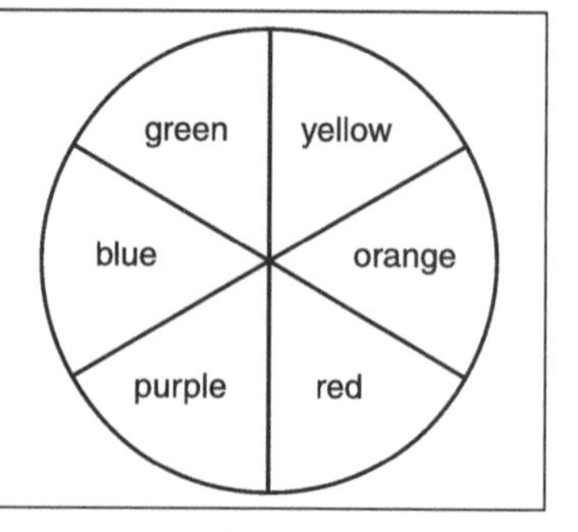

To lighten a colour (a tint) add white. To darken a colour (a shade) add a very small amount of black or some of the complementary colour; this produces a richer shade than by simply adding black.

Weaving

Weaving is a method for producing fabric in which two distinct sets of threads (yarns) are interlaced at right angles. The longitudinal threads are called the warp and the lateral threads are called the weft.

The cloth is woven on a loom, a device to hold the warp threads. The weft is attached to a shuttle which weaves the thread through the warp.

The most common form of weave is the plain weave in which the threads form a simple criss-cross pattern. Each weft thread crosses the warp threads by going over one, then under the next and so on.

'Mandala' is a Sanskrit word roughly translated as 'circle'. It is a ritual symbol in Hinduism and Buddhism to represent the universe.

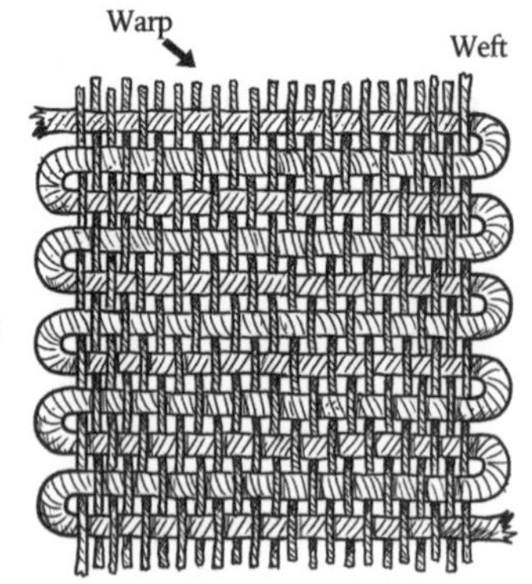

Kandinsky 3D

Wassily Kandinsky (1866–1944) was an influential Russian artist. He is often credited as being the first abstract artist. Recommended website: www.wassilykandinsky.net

Suggested abstract work by Kandinsky:

- *Squares and Concentric Circles* (1913)
- *Swinging* (1925)
- *Circle in a Circle* (1923)
- *Composition VIII* (1923)

Art from other cultures

Scratch paper is made by totally coating sugar paper in oil pastels. It is important to press down hard with the pastels to ensure that it adheres to the paper and that the paper is totally covered in pastels – otherwise the paint will stick to the paper. For the Greek vases, a range of warm colours (red, yellow, orange) should be used. The paper is then covered in black acrylic paint and left to completely dry. Once dry, wooden styluses or sharpened sticks are used to scrape away the paint, this leaves the pastel colours to show through in the desired design/pattern.

Two birds flying high

A bridge with three men, sometimes four,
A willow tree, hanging o'er.
A Chinese temple, there it stands,
Built upon the river sands.
An apple tree, with apples on,
A crooked fence to end my song

Willow Pattern poem, Traditional

Year 6 Long-term planning

Aim 1: Exploring and creating

The National Curriculum states that children should be taught... with creativity, experimentation and an increasing awareness of different kinds of art, craft and design:
- to create sketchbooks to record their observations.

Select and record from first-hand observation and experience.

Use their imagination and originality to explore ideas for different purposes.

Record, annotate and modify work in their sketchbooks by:
- recording from observation, memory and their imagination
- trying out and evaluating their ideas
- designing for a range of different ideas and products.

Children experience and learn about:
- still-life drawing and painting
- the ceramic designs of Clarice Cliff
- drawing and sculpting buildings
- portrait painting
- art from Africa
- sculpture of human figures.

Aim 2: Skills and techniques

The National Curriculum states that children should be taught:
- to develop their techniques, including their control and their use of materials.
- to improve their mastery of art and design techniques, including drawing, painting and sculpture with a range of materials.

To improve their mastery of techniques such as drawing, painting, sculpture and collage with materials such as pencil, charcoal, paint, clay, textiles and ICT. Children develop their artistic techniques in:
- drawing from observation, memory and their imagination
- drawing lines and shape with increasing accuracy, detail and in three dimensions
- creating, drawing and painting still-life compositions
- sculpture using a range of malleable materials
- sculpture using an armature
- creating portraits and caricatures
- creating images using stencil overlays
- tie-dye cloth printing.

Aim 3: Evaluate and analyse

The National Curriculum states that children should be taught:
- to create sketchbooks to record their observations and use them to review and revisit ideas.

Reflect on their own and others' work, comparing ideas and methods and adapting their work accordingly.

Describe how their work might develop further.

Throughout the units of work children should be encouraged to record, annotate and modify their work at all stages of the creative process creating a personal source of information and ideas, including:
- trying out different ideas and designs in their sketchbooks and identifying ways in which their work can be improved upon
- deciding on the best design *from their sketchbook* and using this to inform future work
- using their sketchbook to record *their own work and to include* ideas and work of other artists (this can include photographs, pictures of other works of art, examples of different media and techniques)
- using their sketchbooks to experiment with using different media and practising different skills and techniques.

Aim 4: Art and artists

The National Curriculum states that children should be taught:
- about the greatest artists, architects and designers in history.

The National Curriculum states that children should be taught:
- about the greatest artists, architects and designers in history.

Explore the work of artists, craft makers, and designers working in different times and cultures, including examples selected for them to view and through visits to museums and galleries and on-line collections.

Children learn about the works of a range of artists, including:
- Patrick Caulfield
- Clarice Cliff
- Sue Averall
- Antoni Gaudi
- Julian Opie
- Pablo Picasso
- Andy Warhol
- Anthony Gormley.

Overview of progression in Year 6

Drawing

Throughout their work in Year 6, children are:

- Using sketch books to collect and record visual information and ideas from different sources.
- Working from a variety of sources including observation, photographs and digital images.
- Developing close observation skills, including using view finders.

Through their work in creating a range of still-life drawings, children are:

- Making marks and lines with a wide range of drawing implements including: graphite pencils (5B–5H), pastels (chalk & oil), pens.
- Using different grades of pencil and other implements to create lines, draw different shapes and forms and to produce variations in tone.
- Exploring ways in which surface detail can be added to drawings through applying different patterns and textures, including shading and hatching.
- Beginning to show an awareness of objects having a third dimension.

Through drawing different types of buildings, children are:

- Beginning to show an awareness of objects having a third dimension.
- Using simple perspective in their work using a single focal point and horizon.

Painting

Through creating a range of still-life paintings, children are:

- Creating imaginative work from a variety of sources e.g. observational drawing, themes, inspirational works of art.
- Developing a painting from a drawing, including sketchbook ideas.
- Creating different effects and textures using a range of techniques and paints.
- Using colour to create atmosphere and to show the effect of light.
- Developing an awareness of composition, scale and proportion in their paintings.

Through painting different types of buildings, children are:

- Developing an awareness of composition, scale and proportion in their paintings.
- Using simple perspective in their work using a single focal point and horizon.

Through creating a range of portraits, children are:

- Creating imaginative work from a variety of sources e.g. observational drawing, themes, inspirational works of art.
- Developing a painting from a drawing, including sketchbook ideas.
- Creating different effects and textures using a range of techniques and paints.

Printing

Through creating printed self-portraits, children are:

- Using initial sketchbook ideas to create motifs that are made into printing blocks and stencils.
- Creating different printing effects by using colour overlays.

Year 6 Complete 'Overview of progression' is provided on the CD-ROM, including 'Collage and textiles' and 'Sculpture' objectives.

Medium-term planning: 1. Still life

This unit of work gives children the opportunity to learn about still-life compositions. They learn about how to arrange a composition for effect and begin learning how to create paintings that show light and shade.

W	Outcomes	Objectives	Skills and understanding
1	**Still life 1** • Can create a detailed drawing of a training shoe using a range of drawing pens.	• To respond to what is observed or remembered through drawing • To understand the qualities and effects of a range of drawing media	Understand the genre of 'still life' and discuss with peers. Sketchbooks: Close observation of training shoe or other selected item and detailed drawing skills using different fine line pens.
2	**Still life 2** • Can draw from observation a range of bottles, jars and plates in sketchbooks.	• To respond to what is observed or remembered through drawing • To understand the qualities and effects of a range of drawing media	Sketchbooks: Close observation of a number of objects together and detailed drawing skills. Draw using a range of drawing pencils (5H-5B). Experiment with, and apply, a range of hatching and shading techniques when drawing with pencils.
3	**Still life with paper cut-outs** • Understand how to create a still-life composition using paper cut-outs.	• To respond to what is observed or remembered through drawing • To use sketching to plan a composition	Understand and discuss what makes a good still-life composition (see background information). Using sketchbook designs, children create a number of coloured cut-outs of bottles, jars and plates. Experiment with composition, arranging cut-outs in different ways. Evaluate and improve compositions with peers.
4	**Still life with repeated images** • Can create a still-life painting using repeated images of bottles, jars and plates.	• To mix and match a range of primary and secondary colours • To learn about the work of artists from different times and cultures • To develop an awareness of how paintings are created	Make a number of card cut-outs of bottles, jars and plates. Draw around card cut-outs to create a composition of overlapping images. Block-fill images using only primary and secondary colours to complete the composition.
5	**Still life: In the style of...** • Can create a still-life composition in the style of Patrick Caulfield.	• To respond to what is observed or remembered through drawing • To use sketching to plan a composition • To use painting techniques for different purposes • To mix and match a range of primary and secondary colours • To learn about the work of artists from different times and cultures • To develop an awareness of how paintings are created	Arrange several bottles, jars and plates to create a still-life composition. Sketch still-life composition using drawing pencils. Add blocks of colour to each object in the style of Patrick Caulfield. Finish by drawing outlines of each object using black marker pens.
6	**Still life: Light and shade** • Can show the effect of light and shade when using pastels to create a still-life composition.	• To use sketching to plan a composition • To respond to what is observed or remembered through painting • To understand the qualities and effects of a range of drawing media • To develop an awareness of how paintings are created	Arrange several bottles, jars and plates to create a still-life composition: ensuring that one side of the composition has a dominant light source. Sketch still-life composition using pastels. Add colour to sketch using chalk pastels. Using white and black pastels show the different shades of light reflected in the still life.

Notes:
Sessions 4-5: Look at and discuss images from the work of Patrick Caulfield: Session 4 – *Pottery*, 1969; Session 5 – *Earthenware*, 1967 and *Coloured Still Life*, 1967.

Medium-term planning: 2. Clarice Cliff

In this unit of work, children learn about the work of the English ceramic designer Clarice Cliff. They create their own designs which are transferred on to sculptures that they have made themselves.

W	Outcomes	Objectives	Skills and understanding
1	**Observational drawing** • Can make detailed observational drawings of slices and segments of citrus fruit.	• To develop greater control and confidence in using a range of drawing tools and media • To respond to what is observed or remembered through drawing • To understand the effect of combining different media	Sketchbooks: Close observation of items and detailed drawing skills. Add colour to drawings using watercolour paints.
2	**Clarice Cliff fruit** • Can draw 'stylised' representations of different citrus fruits. • Can design a paper plate using elements of designs by Clarice Cliff.	• To respond to what is observed or remembered through drawing • To understand the effect of combining different media • To create a design for a specific purpose • To learn about the work of artists and designers from different times and cultures	Show images of a range of pottery designs by the artist Clarice Cliff, focus on the range of pottery depicting fruit. Discuss and understand what is meant by the term 'stylised'. Sketchbooks: Design a number of stylised fruits, experimenting and commenting on others' work. Finalised designs are transferred to a paper plate, hand-decorate in the style of Clarice Cliff.
3	**Clarice Cliff bizarre 1** • Can design a circular pattern based on elements of the *Bizarre Collection* by Clarice Cliff.	(As session 2)	Show images of a range of the 'Bizarre' pottery designs by the artist Clarice Cliff. Discuss and identify key features of the design. Produce a range of own designs in sketchbooks.
4	**Clarice Cliff bizarre 2** • Can make a papier-mâché bowl using a mould. • Can decorate a papier-mâché bowl copying a design from a sketchbook.	• To create 3D objects from 2D materials • To design and make for a particular purpose • To create a range of decorative finishes • To understand the importance of using tools appropriately and safely • To apply a range of patterns, textures and decorative finishes to malleable materials	Use a plastic bowl or a plate as a mould; add layers of newspaper, watered down PVA glue, to create a papier-mâché bowl. Add Bizarre designs from previous session, replicated on to the inside of the bowl/plate. Evaluate and improve with input from peers.
5	**Clarice Cliff clay sculpture 1** • Can create a square slab pot. • Can add decorative features in the style of Clarice Cliff.	• To design and make for a particular purpose • To create a range of decorative finishes • To understand the importance of using tools appropriately and safely • To manipulate malleable materials to make 3D sculpture and objects • To blend and join surfaces of malleable materials	Review and discuss a range of ceramics created by Clarice Cliff. Create a square slab pot by joining rolled slabs of clay. Add relief images to the slab pot, in the style of Clarice Cliff, using appropriate techniques to ensure that features adhere to the slab pot.
6	**Clarice Cliff clay sculpture 2** • Can hand-paint and decorate a slab pot in the style of Clarice Cliff.	• To apply a range of patterns, textures and decorative finishes to malleable materials	Add colour to the dried slab pot, made in previous session, using ready-mix/acrylic paint. Experiment with patterns and textures. Finish with clear varnish to seal the colour.

Notes:
Session 4: For the papier-mâché bowls, ensure the inside of the mould is covered with a thin layer of Vaseline before applying several layers of newspaper and thinned PVA glue. Once, dry, cover with a thick layer of white paint (adding matt white emulsion enhances the colour) before adding a final design using acrylic / ready-mix paint.

Medium-term planning: 3. Buildings

In this unit of work, children learn about drawing buildings, in particular in 3D buildings. They study the work of the architect Antoni Gaudi and create a sculpture based on his work.

YEAR 6

W	Outcomes	Objectives	Skills and understanding
1	**Completing the building: 2D** • Can complete a ripped photograph of a famous landmark in two dimensions.	• To develop greater control and confidence in using a range of drawing tools and media • To respond to what is observed or remembered through drawing • To respond to imagination through drawing	Sketchbooks: Ripped photographs of famous landmark buildings (local, national or worldwide) are completed with line drawings. Look for developing skills in observational drawing, using imagination to provide detail when drawing.
2	**Completing the building: 3D** • Can draw cuboids in three dimensions. • Can complete 3D skyscraper pictures using one vanishing point.	• To use simple perspective in their work using focal points and a horizon • To develop skills of drawing 3D objects.	Sketchbooks: Practise drawing cubes and cuboids. Progress to drawing cuboids using one vanishing point. Apply these skills to a 2D cut-out photograph of a skyscraper to create a 3D version in their sketch books.
3	**Sue Averall: Cityscapes 1** • Can sketch and plan out a city landscape using one vanishing point. • Can draw 3D buildings to scale and in proportion.	• To respond to imagination through drawing • To use sketching to plan a composition • To use simple perspective in their work using focal points and a horizon • To learn about the work of artists, architects and designers from different times and cultures	Look at and discuss examples of perspective in artists' work. Focus on how the artist creates the perspective, uses the horizon and creates 3D buildings. Sketch out a cityscape in the style of Sue Averall.
4	**Sue Averall: Cityscapes 2** • Use a range of painting techniques to create aerial perspective. • Can add paint to large blocks of colour and small details when creating a large composition.	• To respond to imagination through painting • To understand the qualities and effects of a range of painting media • To develop an awareness of scale and proportion in their paintings • To develop an awareness of how paintings are created	Working with the cityscape created in previous session, create blue wash colour for the sky using watercolour 'wet on wet'. Add blocks of colour and using different shades of to create depth in composition. Use fine brush skills to add detail to the buildings and surround scenes.
5	**Gaudi in Barcelona 1** • Can create a building sculpture in the style of Gaudi.	• To understand the importance of using tools appropriately and safely • To manipulate malleable materials to make 3D sculpture and objects • To blend and join surfaces of malleable materials • To apply a range of patterns, textures and decorative finishes to malleable materials • To learn about the work of artists from different times and cultures	Look at and discuss the buildings of Antoni Gaudi; how to create a sculpture in this style? Use two slabs of clay to create a base and a free-standing slab from which to sculpt. Use a range of ceramic tools to create 'pull-outs' and 'add-ons' to the sculpture. Use tools to apply patterns and textures to the clay. Use sequins and beads to impress into the sculpture to create patterns and finishes in the style of the architect.
6	**Gaudi in Barcelona 2** • Can apply a paint finish to the sculpture in the style of Antoni Gaudi.	• To create a range of decorative finishes • To apply a range of patterns, textures and decorative finishes to malleable materials	Experiment using a range of paints – acrylic and/or metallic to add a decorative finish to sculptures. Add clear varnish to complete the finish.

Medium-term planning: 4. Portraits

YEAR 6

In this unit of work, children learn about portrait painting and drawing and execute a number of portraits in different styles.

W	Outcomes	Objectives	Skills and understanding
1	**Julian Opie portraits** • Can create their own self-portraits in the style of Julian Opie.	• To use painting techniques for different purposes • To mix and match a range of primary and secondary colours • To learn about the work of artists from different times and cultures • To develop an understanding of portraits and caricature	Discuss and identify the key features of the work of Julian Opie's portraits. Mix paints in order to match skin pigment, then apply to black and white copy of photograph of themselves to create a self-portrait in the style of Julian Opie. When dry, complete the portraits with thick black outlines – in the Opie style.
2	**Drawing a face** • Can draw a human face in proportion.	• To develop an understanding of portraits and caricature	Understand and apply relevant techniques to draw a human face in proportion, including: • Different shapes of face. • Shape and position of the eyes, nose and mouth relative to each other. • Relative position, shape and size of the ears. • Adding fine details: eyelashes, eyebrows, nostrils.
3	***Dora Maar* by Pablo Picasso** • Can draw a front-view and a side-view portrait of the same person in proportion. • Can use both images to create a portrait painting in the style of *Dora Maar* by Pablo Picasso.	• To develop an understanding of portraits and caricature	Sketchbooks: Draw front-view and side-view portraits of self or other person. Draw round portraits with thick marker pen. Cut out both portraits and cut into pieces; combine pieces from both to create one portrait. Add colour using acrylic paints.
4	**Self-caricatures** • Can create a caricature of themselves from a self-portrait photograph.	• To develop an understanding of portraits and caricature • To develop greater control and confidence in using a range of drawing tools and media • To create a design for a specific purpose	Understand that a caricature looks like the person, but alters and exaggerates their features. Using a traced line drawing of a photograph, alter and exaggerate certain features to create a caricature. Consider: • exaggerated hair, eyebrows thicker • chin narrower or squarer • cheeks wider, nose, lips and or smile bigger. Photocopy finished caricature and add colour.
5 & 6	**Andy Warhol inspired prints** • Can create a set of stencils from a self-portrait. • Can overlay a series of stencils to create multi-coloured self-portraits in the style of Andy Warhol.	• To develop an understanding of portraits and caricature • To know that making a print involves transferring an image from one surface to another • To know that the printing process can result in repeated images • To understand and apply a range of printmaking processes	Display work of Andy Warhol and discuss. Take two sessions to create an Andy Warhol print. • Trace self-portrait photograph using tracing paper and black markers to create an outline drawing. • Make five photocopies of the outline drawing (preferably on to white card). • For each colour (maximum of five) an outline copy is taken and the area to be printed is cut out to form a stencil. Suggestions are: Colour 1: Skin Colour 4: Eyes, eyebrows, nose Colour 2: Hair Colour 5: Lips Colour 3: Torso Use stencils to create a self-portrait print on coloured paper – use masking tape to make sure that all stencils are aligned in position.

Notes:
Sessions 5–6: Can easily be adapted for screen printing.
Julian Opie is a modern British visual artist. He is well-known for his artwork for the 'Blur: The Best Of' album cover. He has produced a range of portraits for which his style is instantly recognisable. www.julianopie.com.
Pablo Picasso: Dora Maar was the inspiration for many of Picasso's portraits in which she is portrayed both from the side and from the front.

Medium-term planning: 5. Art from Africa

YEAR 6

In this unit of work, the theme of art from Africa is used to consolidate learning in sculpture, textiles and printing and to teach the technique of tie-dye.

W	Outcomes	Objectives	Skills and understanding
1	**African mask design** • Can design an African mask after studying a range of images. • Can create a symmetrical African mask design using coloured paper.	• To respond to what is observed or remembered through drawing • To create a design for a specific purpose • To combine a range of materials to create a collage	Sketchbooks: Design a symmetrical African mask using line drawing, using a range of images to inform the design. Using paper cut-out technique, recreate the mask design using coloured sugar paper (links with Year 4 Matisse unit).
2	**African mask sculpture 1** • Can create an African ceramic mask using a range of techniques and tools.	• To manipulate malleable materials to make 3D sculpture and objects • To blend and join surfaces of malleable materials	Create a basic ceramic mask shape by rolling clay and shaping over a ball of newspaper. Create features on the mask by cutting away and joining pieces of clay to create prominent features such as the mouth, nose, eyebrows, ears and hair. Use a range of ceramic tools to create patterns, texture and design features on the mask.
3	**African mask sculpture 2** • Can add decorative paint and finishes to an African ceramic mask.	• To apply a range of patterns, textures and decorative finishes to malleable materials	Apply a range of paint and decorative finishes to the ceramic mask created in previous session that reflect traditional African mask designs. Apply a background colour of dark brown and then use white, yellow ochre and orange to complete the decoration. Apply a clear varnish to the decorated mask. Compare finished masks with images of traditional African masks.
4	**Tie-dye** • Can create a decorative piece of cloth using tie-dye methods.	• To decorate fabrics in a number of different ways and finishes • To use dyes, paints, batik, appliqué, etc. to make a textile design	Research a range of African clothed designs from many different countries. Discuss and identify features particular to countries or peoples. Use tie-dye techniques to create a pattern on a squared piece of cloth by either: • bunching • knotting • spiralling • tubing. Immerse the cloth in a bucket of dye and leave for 15 minutes.
5	**Printing the cloth** • Can create a decorative border on cloth using an impressed method.	• To decorate fabrics in a number of different ways and finishes • To use dyes, paints, batik, appliqué, etc. to make a textile design	Looking back to research into a range of African clothes in last session, focus on those with repeating patterned borders. Use impress printing method by creating a pattern design on a small square of polystyrene foam. Create repeated pattern design on tie-dye cloth using fabric paint as an ink.
6	**Adding the detail** • Can add an African-inspired central motif to a piece of cloth.	• To decorate fabrics in a number of different ways and finishes. • To use dyes, paints, batik, appliqué, etc. to make a textile design	Sketchbooks: Design an African silhouette scene. Transfer design on to the centre of printed tie-dye cloth using black fabric pens/paint with black fabric paint.

Notes:
Digital art: Designs for the mask and for the repeating border pattern can be created using paint software.

Medium-term planning: 6. Action figures

In this unit of work, children learn about creating human sculpture figures by creating an armature and then covering with malleable materials to give the sculpture form.

W	Outcomes	Objectives	Skills and understanding
1	**Stick figures in action** • Can draw a human figure in action by drawing stick figures.	• To respond to what is observed or remembered through drawing • To use sketching to plan a composition • To create a design for a specific purpose	Show how to create simple stick figure in proportion, including major joints of arms and legs. Display images of different sports people in action and discuss how the major joints appear in each. Sketchbooks: Create simple stick figures and experiment with drawing different figures in action.
2	**Anthony Gormley** • Can create a simple human figure armature for a sculpture. • Can apply plaster bandages on to an armature to create a human figure.	• To manipulate malleable materials to make 3D sculpture and objects • To apply a range of patterns, textures and decorative finishes to malleable materials	Show a range of images of human figure sculptures by the artist Anthony Gormley. Use thin wire to create a simple stick man as an armature for sculpture. Attach armature to block of wood to provide stable base for sculpture. Use plaster bandages (mod-roc) to create form for the sculpture. Finish with metallic paint when dry.
3	**Action figure design** • Can draw a design for a human form in an action pose.	• To respond to what is observed or remembered through drawing • To use sketching to plan a composition • To create a design for a specific purpose	From a range of photographs, choose an image of a figure in action then: • Draw stick figure. • Add ovals to create a solid human figure, experimenting with further poses of the figure in action. • Draw finished sculpture, including application of colour.
4	**Action figure armature** • Can create an armature for a sculpture of an action figure.	• To design and make for a particular purpose • To understand the importance of using tools appropriately and safely • To manipulate malleable materials to make 3D sculpture and objects	Using stick figure drawing from session 3 as a guide, create an armature out of thin wire of the figure in action. Make simple figure first, then create one or more action poses. Chosen armature is attached to base block of wood.
5	**Solid action figure** • Can apply a malleable material to an armature to create a posed sculpture.	• To use a range of adhesive and joining techniques when creating sculpture • To understand the importance of using tools appropriately and safely • To manipulate malleable materials to make 3D sculpture and objects	Using solid figure drawing from session 3 as a guide, pack the armature with newspaper to create the oval shapes – secure in place using masking tape. Complete sculpture by adding layers of papier-mâché to create a smooth finish.
6	**Finishing the figure** • Can apply paint to complete a sculpture of an action figure. • Can follow a design in a sketchbook to complete a sculpture.	• To apply a range of patterns, textures and decorative finishes to malleable materials	Apply detailed paintwork to the sculpture following the design from session 3. Display and discuss sculptures with peers.

Notes:

Session 2: Suitable images of human figures to illustrate the work of Anthony Gormley include: *Another Place* or *Event Horizon*.

As a development of session 2 featuring Anthony Gormley, *The Angel of the North* could be studied as a piece of public art and the focus of the sculpture work could be modified accordingly. Visit www.scholastic.co.uk/100artanddesign for a useful glossary of all the key terms related to sculpture used in this and other units.

Year 6 Background knowledge

Still life

Patrick Caulfield was a British artist and printmaker known for his bold use of colours and simplistic designs.

Images of his work can be found on the BBC Website 'Your Paintings'.

Composition: The key to composition is variety – do not make any two things the same. This can apply to shape, colour, size and the gaps between objects. There should be areas of light and dark, particularly in the background. The background should be plain and simple so as not to detract from the focus objects in the composition.

(www.nga.gov/kids/zone/stilllife.htm is an excellent website for teaching children about placing objects in a still-life composition.)

Clarice Cliff

Clarice Cliff was a British ceramics artist who worked from the 1930s through to the 1960s. She created designs for the ceramic pottery works around Stoke-on-Trent. Her designs very much reflect the Art Deco period in which she worked. One of her most famous collections was called 'Bizarre' which used geometric shapes in bold patterns combined with bold colours.

www.claricecliff.co.uk or www.claricecliff.com

Buildings

Session 1: Provide copies of coloured photographs of landmark buildings that have been ripped vertically in half. (If possible provide photographs in which the buildings are symmetrically built – St Paul's Cathedral, Tower Bridge and Buckingham Palace are obvious London landmarks that can be used.)

Session 2: The photographs are cut-outs of the fronts of skyscraper buildings to complete.

Portraits

When drawing faces, the key points to note for children are:

- In general, the face is an oval shape not round. (This can be extended to look at different facial shapes; long, heart-shaped, squared jaw etc.)
- The eyes are drawn half way down the face and the distance between the eyes is the same width as one of the eyes. The bottom of the nose is the same as the distance between the eyes.
- The tops of the ears are at the same height as the eyes.
- The neck is nearly the same width as the head.

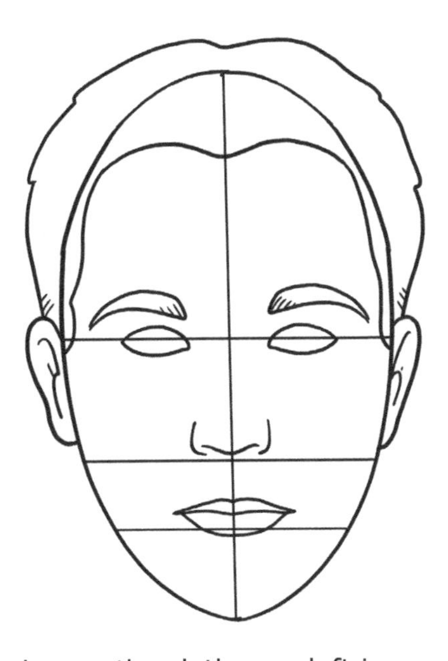

Art from Africa

Tie-dye: Cold water dyes can be used for the dyeing process. The longer the cloths are left in the dye, the stronger the colour will become. To create the different designs, allow children to experiment with rubber bands and marbles when knotting the cloth.

Action figures

Modelling wire is best used when creating armatures for sculpture as it is flexible enough for children to be able to manipulate it whilst retaining its strength to maintain its basic shape when a malleable material is applied. Anthony Gormley is a famous contemporary British sculpture best known for *The Angel of the North* and for his series of human sculptures in public places.

www.anthonygormley.com

Progression in art & design at Key Stage 1

Children should have the opportunity to:
- Make and record observations, first-hand and from memory.
- Develop their ideas, try things out and ask questions.
- Explore thoughts and ideas using their experience and imagination and originality through a range of creative approaches.
- Learn about, understand and value the work of artists, craft makers and designers; the differences and similarities between them and making links to their own works.
- Reflect on what they and others have done and say what they think and feel about it and suggest ways in which they might change or develop their work.
- Work safely with a range of tools and techniques, including appropriate new technology tools, taking care of themselves and others.

Drawing	Painting	Printing
Draw on different surfaces with a range of media including: • pencils • crayons • pastels • felt-tipped pens • charcoal • chalk. Experiment to create different lines and marks made with a range of media. Draw lines and shapes from observations of nature and objects. Investigate tone by drawing lines, shapes and patterns of different shades of light and dark. Investigate textures by copying patterns and making rubbings.	Use a variety of paint media and experiment to produce a range of effects. Use a variety of tools and techniques including different brushes and investigate the kinds of marks which can be made. Identify primary colours and undertake simple colour-mixing to include shades and tones. Identify primary colours and mix primary shades and tones. Match colours to artefacts and objects. Name different types of paint and their properties.	Use a range of found objects to make prints. Experiment with mono-printing. Create simple printing blocks using press printing techniques. Make printed images through rubbing (frottage). Create different simple designs by: • repeating patterns • overprinting.

Progression in art & design at Key Stage 1, continued

Children should have the opportunity to:
- Make and record observations, first-hand and from memory.
- Develop their ideas, try things out and ask questions.
- Explore thoughts and ideas using their experience and imagination and originality through a range of creative approaches.
- Learn about, understand and value the work of artists, craft makers and designers; the differences and similarities between them and making links to their own works.
- Reflect on what they and others have done and say what they think and feel about it and suggest ways in which they might change or develop their work.
- Work safely with a range of tools and techniques, including appropriate new technology tools, taking care of themselves and others.

Sculpture	Collage	Textiles
Shaping malleable materials in a variety of ways including squeezing, rolling, flattening and pinching. Manipulate malleable materials for a purpose: • pinch pot • slab tile. Impressing different textures and patterns using a variety of objects. Modelling, constructing and joining recycled, natural and man-made materials. Investigate different joining techniques.	Use a range of media to create images, including: • tissue paper • crêpe paper • magazine photographs • textiles • photocopies • textured papers. Sort and group materials for different purposes e.g. colour, image, texture. Arrange and glue materials to different backgrounds. Create an image using collage. Fold, crumple, tear and overlap papers.	Cut and shape fabric using scissors. Apply fabric shapes with glue or by stitching. Apply decoration using beads, buttons, sequins, feathers etc. Change and modify threads and fabrics, knotting, fraying, fringing, knitting, twisting, plaiting. Apply colour to fabrics through: • printing • painting • dipping • crayoning. Create fabrics by weaving materials.

Progression in art & design at Key Stage 2

Children should have the opportunity to:

- Select and record from first hand observation and experience using imagination and originality to explore ideas for different purposes.
- Record, annotate and modify work in their sketchbook.
- Develop their skills and techniques, including their control and confidence, to be able to work independently and purposefully, and to collaborate in teams.
- Explore, understand and value the work of artists, crafts people, and designers working in different times and cultures, including examples selected for them to view and through visits to museums and galleries and online collections.
- Reflect on their own and others' work, comparing ideas and methods and adapt their work accordingly. Then describe how they might develop it further.
- Work safely using tools, equipment, materials and techniques appropriate to the task, including appropriate new technology tools.

Drawing	Painting	Printing
Use sketchbooks to collect and record visual information and ideas from different sources. Work from a variety of sources including observation, photographs and digital images. Develop close observation skills, including using view finders. Make marks and lines with a wide range of drawing implements including: • graphite pencil (5B–5H) • charcoal • colouring pencils • wax crayons • pastels (chalk & oil) • pens. Use different grades of pencil and other implements to create lines, draw different shapes and forms and to produce variations in tone. Explore ways in which surface detail can be added to drawings through applying different patterns and textures, including shading and hatching. Begin to show an awareness of objects having a third dimension. Use simple perspective in their work using a single focal point and horizon.	Create imaginative work from a variety of sources e.g. observational drawing, themes, inspirational works of art. Develop a painting from a drawing, including sketchbook ideas. Create different effects and textures using a range of techniques and paints: • blocking in colour • washes • thickened paint. Extended knowledge of colour theory: • primary and secondary • tints, tones and shades • complementary and contrasting. Using colour to create atmosphere and to show the effect of light. Develop an awareness of composition, scale and proportion in their paintings. Use simple perspective in their work using a single focal point and horizon.	Create printing blocks using a relief or impressed method. Using initial sketchbook ideas to create motifs that are made into printing blocks. Create different printing effects by using: • repeating patterns • block rotation • colour overlays.

Progression in art & design at Key Stage 2, continued

Children should have the opportunity to:

- Select and record from first hand observation and experience using imagination and originality to explore ideas for different purposes.
- Record, annotate and modify work in their sketchbook.
- Develop their skills and techniques, including their control and confidence, to be able to work independently and purposefully, and to collaborate in teams.
- Explore, understand and value the work of artists, crafts people, and designers working in different times and cultures, including examples selected for them to view and through visits to museums and galleries and online collections.
- Reflect on their own and others' work, comparing ideas and methods and adapt their work accordingly. Then describe how they might develop it further.
- Work safely using tools, equipment, materials and techniques appropriate to the task, including appropriate new technology tools.

Sculpture	Collage	Textiles
Plan and design sculptures from observation or imagination using sketchbook ideas. Use recycled, natural and man-made materials to create sculptures including: • cardboard • clay • papier-mâché. Develop skills in using clay including: • slab and clay pots • relief tiles • modelling • joining. Create patterns and textures when using malleable materials such as clay.	Use collage as a means of expression from sketchbook ideas. Use a range of media to create collages. Experiment with a range of collage techniques such as: • tearing • overlapping • layering to create images and textures. Add collage to a painted, printed or drawn background.	Experience a range of textile techniques such as: • printing • dyeing • weaving • stitching • paste resist • batik to create different textural effects. Create 3D structures from different textiles. Develop skills in using tools to manipulate textiles through stitching, cutting, joining. Apply a range of decorative finishes to provide detail and to enhance the textile.

SCHOLASTIC

Available in this series:

100 English Lessons

Year 1 – 978-1407-12759-0
Year 2 – 978-1407-12760-6
Year 3 – 978-1407-12761-3
Year 4 – 978-1407-12762-0
Year 5 – 978-1407-12763-7
Year 6 – 978-1407-12764-4

100 Computing Lessons

Years 1–2 – 978-1407-12856-6
Years 3–4 – 978-1407-12857-3
Years 5–6 – 978-1407-12858-0

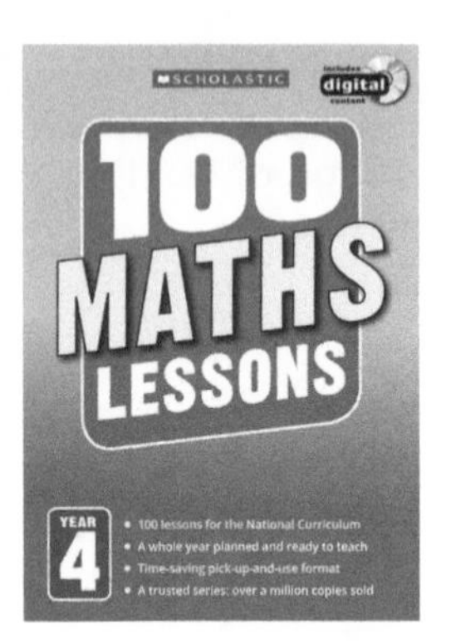

100 Maths Lessons

Year 1 – 978-1407-12771-2
Year 2 – 978-1407-12772-9
Year 3 – 978-1407-12773-6
Year 4 – 978-1407-12774-3
Year 5 – 978-1407-12775-0
Year 6 – 978-1407-12776-7

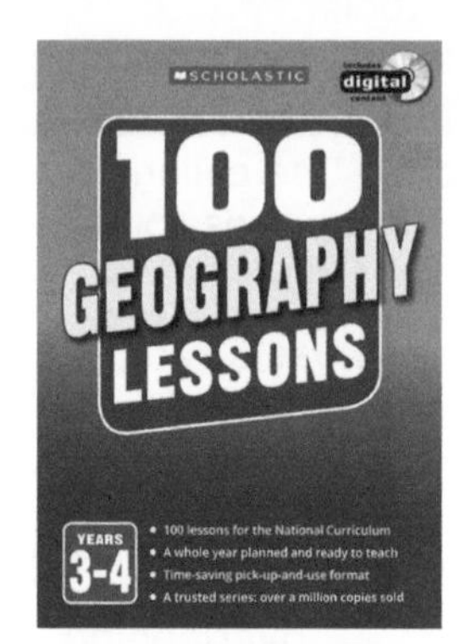

100 Geography Lessons

Years 1–2 – 978-1407-12850-4
Years 3–4 – 978-1407-12851-1
Years 5–6 – 978-1407-12852-8

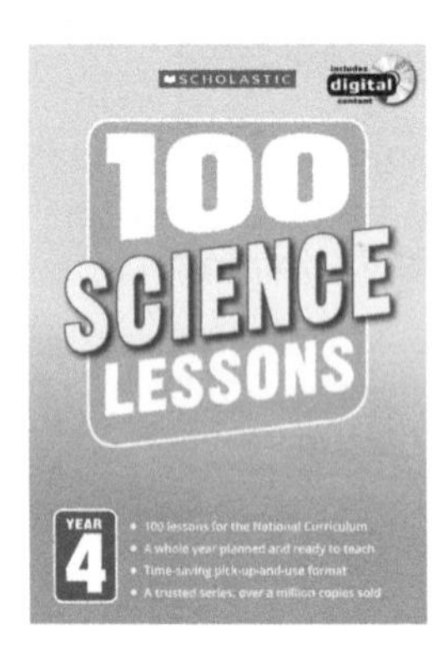

100 Science Lessons

Year 1 – 978-1407-12765-1
Year 2 – 978-1407-12766-8
Year 3 – 978-1407-12767-5
Year 4 – 978-1407-12768-2
Year 5 – 978-1407-12769-9
Year 6 – 978-1407-12770-5

100 History Lessons

Years 1–2 – 978-1407-12853-5
Years 3–4 – 978-1407-12854-2
Years 5–6 – 978-1407-12855-9

---

100 Lessons Planning Guides

100 English Lessons
Planning Guide
978-1407-12839-9

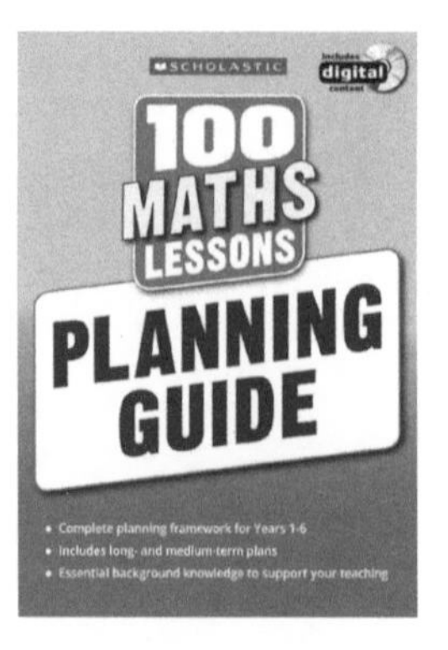

100 Maths Lessons
Planning Guide
978-1407-12840-5

100 Science Lessons
Planning Guide
978-1407-12841-2

To find out more, call: **0845 603 9091** or visit **www.scholastic.co.uk/100lessons**

Aims	Key Stage 1
	Year 1 / Year 2
Exploring and creating: Produce creative work, exploring their ideas and recording their experiences.	Children should be taught: ✔ to use a range of materials creatively to design a make products ✔ to use drawing, painting and sculpture to develop share their ideas, experiences and imagination.

SCHOLASTIC

& DESIGN IN THE URRICULUM

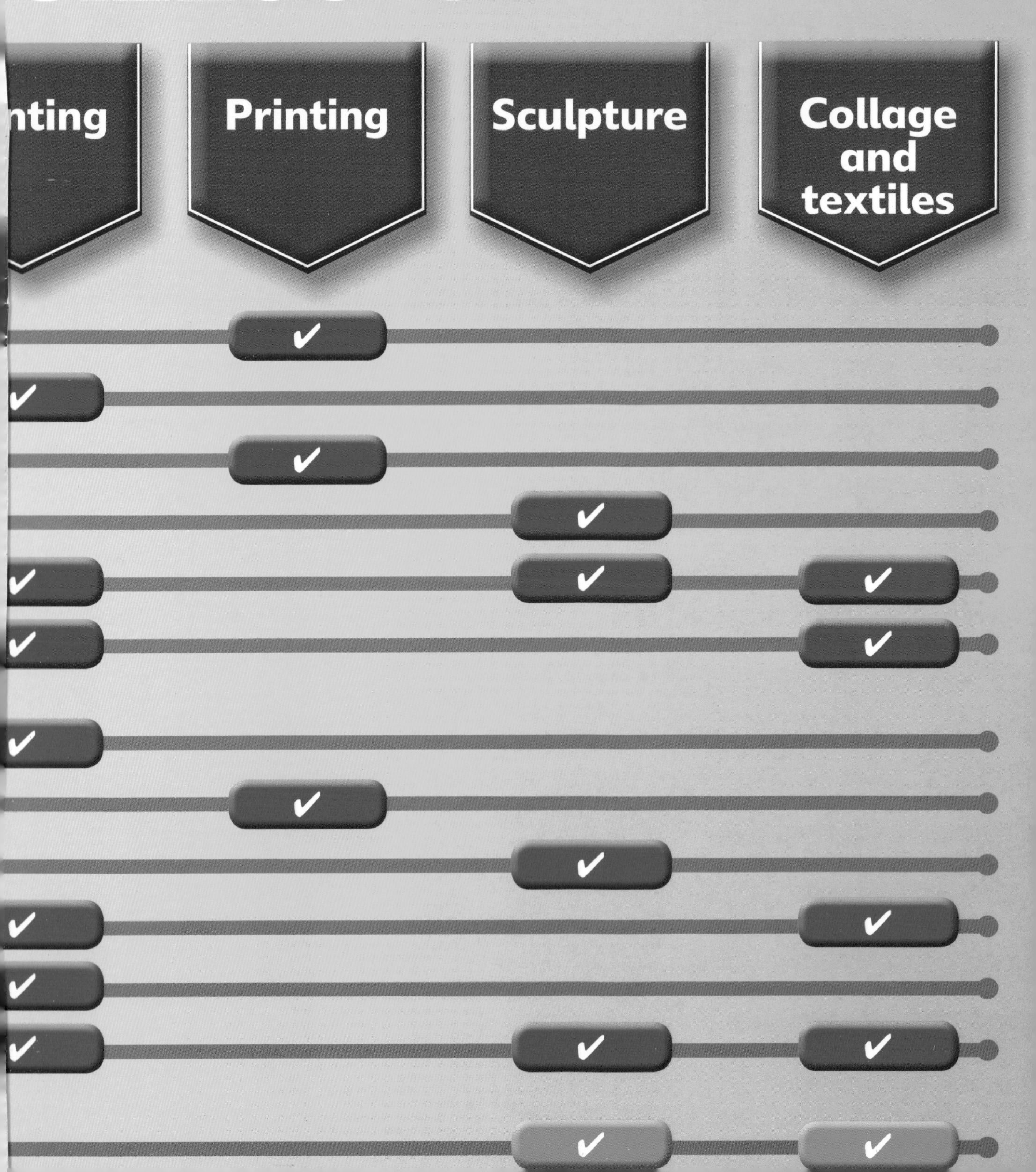

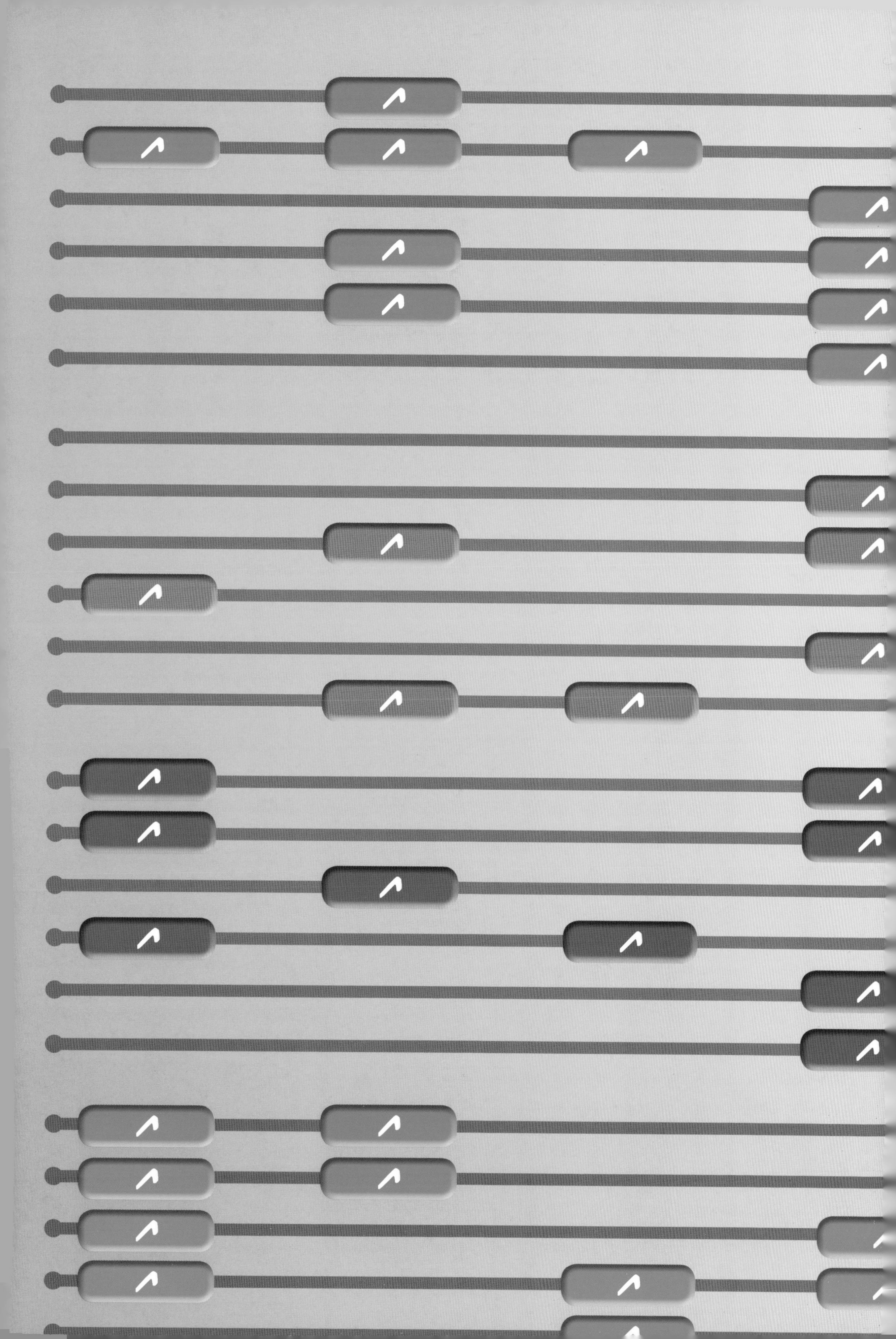

Skills and techniques: Become proficient in using drawing, painting, sculpture and other creative expressions.

Children should be taught:

- ✔ to develop a wide range of art and design technic in using colour, pattern, texture, line, shape, form and space.

Evaluate and analyse: Evaluate and analyse artistic works using the language of art, craft and design.

Children should be taught:

- ✔ to use drawing, painting and sculpture to develo share their ideas, experiences and imagination.

Art and artists: Know about the great artists, craft makers and designers, and understand the historical development of their art forms.

Children should be taught:

- ✔ about the work of artists, craft makers and desig describing the differences and similarities betwee different practices and disciplines, and making lin their own work.

ues

Children should be taught:

- ✔ to improve their mastery of art and design techniques, such as drawing, painting and sculpture with materials (e.g. pencil, charcoal, paint, clay)
- ✔ to develop their techniques, including their control and their use of materials.

and

Children should be taught:

- ✔ to use their sketch books to record observations and use them to review and revisit ideas.

ers,

to

Children should be taught:

- ✔ about the greatest artists, architects and designers in history.

Year	Unit	
Year 3	3: Van Gogh	
	4: Savannah!	✔
	5: Celtic crafts	
	6: Wild things	✔
Year 4	1: Doodles	✔
	2: Landscapes	
	3: Matisse – Painting with scissors	
	4: Masquerade	
	5: Heraldry	✔
	6: Rainforests	
Year 5	1: William Morris	
	2: Blossoming out	✔
	3: Weaving	
	4: Kandinsky 3D	
	5: Art from other cultures	✔
	6: Mapping it out	✔
Year 6	1: Still life	✔
	2: Clarice Cliff	
	3: Buildings	✔
	4: Portraits	✔
	5: Art from Africa	
	6: Action figures	✔

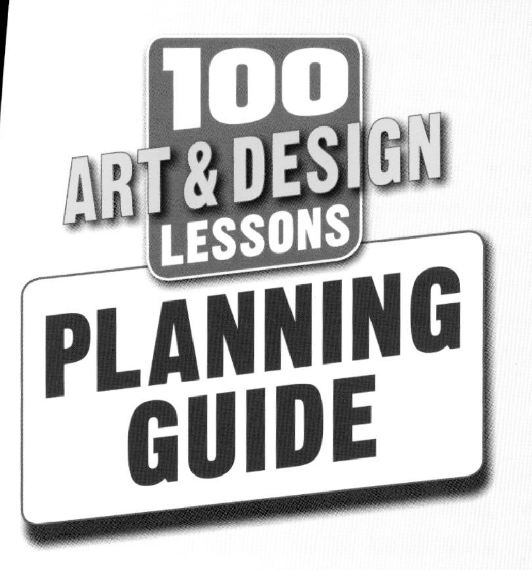

ART & C

	Topic	Drawing	Pa
Year 1	1: Weather	✔	
	2: Gardens	✔	
	3: From the toybox		
	4: Bugs and beetles		
	5: Fireworks	✔	
	6: Under the sea	✔	
Year 2	1: Victoriana	✔	
	2: Vegetable and fruit printing		
	3: Straight-line and curvy sculpture		
	4: *Elmer* the elephant	✔	
	5: Paul Klee	✔	
	6: At the seaside	✔	
	1: Down our street	✔	

SCHOLASTIC

DESIGN IN THE
RRICULUM

nd

and

Children should be taught:

- ✔ to create sketch books to record their observations and use them to review and revisit ideas
- ✔ to experiment and become increasingly aware of different kinds of art, craft and design.